RIDER WAITE SMITH TAROT
Symbols and Cheat Sheets

DISCLAIMER

"Please note that the interpretations of tarot symbols provided in this cheat sheet are intended for informational and entertainment purposes only. Tarot readings are subjective and should not be relied upon for making significant decisions or replacing professional advice.

The meanings of tarot cards can vary widely based on individual perspectives and contexts. Always use your judgment and consider seeking guidance from qualified professionals for matters related to health, finance, or legal issues."

INDEX

DIFFERENCES BETWEEN CARD TYPES
Cheat Sheet

MAJOR ARCANA
Life lessons

The Major Arcana consists of 22 cards that represent significant life events, spiritual lessons, and deep, impactful themes.

TAROT SUITS
Current Situation

The Minor Arcana includes 56 cards divided into four suits: Cups, Pentacles, Swords, and Wands. These cards focus on day-to-day activities and practical aspects of life, such as emotions, work, challenges, and personal growth.

COURT CARDS
Past or present

The court cards do not have specific numbers associated with them. They are considered a separate category in the tarot, and their roles are more nuanced.

PAGE

Represents youthful energy, curiosity, and a learning mindset. It often signifies the beginning or exploration of a particular aspect related to the suit.

The Page may also indicate messages, news, or the introduction of new ideas.

KNIGHT

Embodies action, movement, and a dynamic approach. It signifies progression, challenges, and the need for initiative.

The Knight often represents the pursuit of goals, adventure, and the determination to overcome obstacles.

QUEEN

Associated with maturity, nurturing, and emotional intelligence. It signifies a supportive and compassionate presence, offering guidance and understanding.

The Queen may represent individuals or aspects related to relationships, intuition, and empathy.

KING

Embodies authority, leadership, and mastery. It represents a mature and responsible approach to the energies of the suit.

The King often signifies stability, competence, and the wise application of knowledge or resources.

HOW TO READ MINORS CARDS
Cheat Sheet

Cups
Suit

Pentacles
Suit

Swords
Suit

Wands
Suit

Water

Earth

Air

Fire

Emotional
Emotions, health, creativity relationships, intuition and compassion.

Physical
Material wealth, career, finances, business and possessions.

Mental
Mind and intellect, action, knowledge, power and change.

Spiritual
Will power and life force, energy, passion, creativity, ego and personality.

QUICK TIP TO READ MINOR SUITS

Each suit represents a particular theme or area of life, with the individual cards within that suit reflecting variations on those central concepts.

Suit — Current situation

Suit Meaning + Number Meaning = Card Meaning

Court Card — People in your life | Past or Present

Suit Meaning + Court Card Meaning = Card Meaning

**1	Ace**	Beginnings, potential, new opportunities.
**2	Two**	Balance, duality, partnerships, choices.
**3	Three**	Growth, creativity, collaboration.
**4	Four**	Stability, structure, foundation.
**5	Five**	Change, conflict, instability, challenge
**6	Six**	Harmony, balance, resolution.
**7	Seven**	Strategy, introspection, reflection, spirituality.
**8	Eight**	Power, progress, movement.
**9	Nine**	Fulfillment, nearing completion, introspection.
**10	Ten**	Completion, culmination, new cycles.

COURT CARDS

Page — Represent beginnings, learning, and messages. Children or young people

Knight — Symbolize action, adventure, and movement. Young adult.

Queen — Represent nurturing, authority, and intuition. mature women

King — Symbolize mastery, authority, and control. mature male

The fool	Trust	**Wheel of Fortune**	External changes
The magician	Skill	**Justice**	Fair treatment
The High Priestess	Wisdom	**The Hanged Man**	Sacrifice, waiting
The Empress	Connecting mind and body	**Death**	Change
The Emperor	Logic	**Temperance**	Patience
The Hierophant	Tradition	**The Devil**	Inner demons
The Lovers	Self-love, passion	**The Tower**	Upheaval
The Chariot	Direction	**The Star**	Hope
Strength	Inner strength	**The Moon**	Emotional turmoil
The Hermit	Solitude	**The Sun**	Joy
		Judgement	Evaluation
		The World	Success

 Cups *Suit*  Pentacles *Suit*   Swords *Suit*   Wands *Suit*

 Emotional   Physical   Mental   Spiritual

Emotional	Physical	Mental	Spiritual
1 Emotional growth	1 New money	1 New focus	1 New energy
2 Love	2 Making ends meet	2 Decision	2 Contemplation
3 Friendships	3 Working with others	3 Sorrow	3 Seeking direction
4 Offers	4 Solidity	4 Rest	4 Happy home life
5 Grief	5 Lack	5 Deception	5 Arguments
6 Inner child	6 Generosity	6 Escape	6 Success
7 Illusions	7 Building	7 Worries	7 Competition
8 Turning away	8 Hard work	8 Restriction	8 Quick developments
9 Emotional satisfaction	9 Refinement	9 Sleepless nights	9 Defense
10 Inner peace	10 Satisfaction	10 Exhaustion	10 Burdens

Page	Naivety	**Page**	Magnetism	**Page**	Talent	**Page**	Charisma
Knight	Romanticism	**Knight**	Caution	**Knight**	Restlessness	**Knight**	Daring
Queen	Caring	**Queen**	Cleverness	**Queen**	Independence	**Queen**	Strength
King	Expression	**King**	Responsibility	**King**	Invention	**King**	Creation

SYMBOLS IN RIDER WAITE SMITH DECK
Cheat Sheet

Birds

Freedom
Ascension
Messengers

Bull
Power
Stamina
Stability

Butterfly

Beauty
Rebirth
Transformation

Cat

Magic
Nobility
Sensuality

Crab
Defensive
Adaptable
Resilience

Crow

Power
Mystery
Intuition

Dog

Loyalty
Protection
Friendship

Dove
Love
Peace
Renewal

Eagle

Wisdom
Freedom
Perception

Fish

Emotion
Intuition
Creativity

Fox

Playful
Cunning
Resourceful

Goat

Growth
Balance
Persistence

Horse

Travel
Power
Freedom

Lamb

Purity
Innocence
Gentleness

Lion
Control
Courage
Strenght

Lizard
Vision
Expansion
Regeneration

Owl

Change
Wisdom
Intuition

Rabbit

Fertility
Sexuality
Good Luck

Ram

Strength
Leadership
Determination

Scorpion

Change
Mystery
Survival

Snake

Desire
Rebirth
Temptation

Spider

Growth
Mastery
Creativity

Turtle

Wisdom
Longevity
Protection

Wolf
Loyalty
Courage
Freedom

Angel

Clarity
Guidance
Protection

Blindfold

Denial
Barriers
Resistance

Boat

Travel
Movement
Subconcious

Books

Growth
Learning
Knowledge

Castle

Goals
Safety
Achievement

Crown

Status
Authority
Expression

Cups
Intuition
Emotions
Relationships

Fire
Power
Passion
Creativity

Keys

Wisdom
Intellect
Freedom

Lantern

Clarity
Guidance
Inner-knowing

Lightning

Change
Message
Intervention

Moon

Illusion
Emotions
Uncounscious

Mountains

Challenges
Endurance
Obstructions

Pentacles

Money
Career
Possessions

Rainbow

Love
Hope
Fulfillment

Rose
Faith
Beauty
Beginnings

Scale

Justice
Balance
Fairness

Sun

Vitality
Creativity
Development

Sunflower

Joy
Peace
Friendship

Swords

Action
Knowledge
Communication

Tree

Growth
Stability
Protection

Wands
Ego
Passion
Life Force

Water
Healing
Creativity
Reflection

Wreath

Peace
Victory
Security

PLANETS CORRESPONDENCES
Cheat Sheet

SUN

"I AM"

Ego, Vitality, Purpose, Life Force, Consciousness, Masculine Energy.

Heart, Back, Spine, Left Eye, Blood Circulation.

 Rules the 5th House.

 Leo

MOON

"I FEEL"

Habit, Security, Instincts, Emotions, Receptivity, Feminine Energy.

Female Reproductive Organs, Breast, Digestion, Right Eye, Right Arm.

Rules the 4th House.

Cancer

MERCURY

"I THINK"

Reason, Intellect, Movement, Expression, Transportation, Communication.

Nervous System, Brain, Respiratory Functions.

Rules the 3rd & 6th House.

Gemini Virgo

VENUS

"I LOVE"

Love, Beauty, Creation, Pleasure, Romance, Sensuality.

Thyroid Gland, Left Arm, Throat, Kidneys, Lower Back.

Rules the 2nd & 7th House.

Taurus Libra

MARS

"I ACT"

Action, Energy, Conflict, Passion, Sex Drive, Aggression.

Sex Glands, Left Ear, Muscular System.

Rules the 1st House.

Aries

JUPITER

"I GROW"

Religion, Optimism, Good Luck, Expansion, Philosophy, Abondance.

Pituitary Gland, Function of the Liver.

 Rules the 9th House.

Sagittarius

URANUS

"I ACHIEVE"

Honor, Wisdom, Ambition, Structure, Discipline, Restriction.

Skin, Teeth, Bones, Gallbladder, Spleen, Right Ear.

Rules the 10th House.

Capricorn

SATURN

"I EVOLVE"

Freedom, Progress, Rebellion, Awakening, Originality, Sudden Change.

Pineal Gland, Gonads, Blood System.

Rules the 11th House.

Aquarius

NEPTUNE

"I DREAM"

Dreams, Illusion, Intuition, Sensitivity, Spirituality, Psychic Ability.

Area of Thalamus, in the Nervous System.

Rules the 12th House.

Pisces

PLUTO

"I EMPOWER"

Sex, Death, Obsession, Underworld, Regeneration, Subconscious.

Reproductive Function, Gonad, Cell Production.

Rules the 8th House.

Scorpio

ZODIAC CORRESPONDENCES
Cheat Sheet

ARIES

Mar 21 | Apr 19

Courageous, Passionate, Direct, Naive, Aggressive, Egotistical

Colors
Red, Scarlet

Rules the 1st House of
Self

Fire

Carnelian, Bloodstone, Red Jasper

Basil, Ginger, Garlic

TAURUS

Apr 20 | May 20

Persistent, Dependable, Powerful, Stubborn, Possessive, Materialistic

Colors
Green, Pink

Rules the 2nd House of
Possessions

Earth

Rose Quartz, Emerald, Jade

Thyme, Sage, Mint

GEMINI

May 21 | June 20

Energetic, Playful, Wise, Restless, Two-faced, Judgmental

Colors
Yellow, Light Green

Rules the 3rd House of
Communication

Air

Agate, Citrine, Tiger's Eye

Lavender, Dill, Marjoram

CANCER

Jun 21 | Jul 22

Protective, Creative, Intuitive, Loyal, Moody, Selfish, Clingy

Colors
Silver, White

Rules the 4th House of
Home

Water

Moonstone, Pearl, Selenite

Chamomile, Lemon Balm, Mugwort

LEO

Jul 23 | Aug 22

Vivacious, Brave, Protective, Controlling, Stubborn, Vain

Colors
Gold, Orange

Rules the 5th House of
Pleasure

Fire

Sunstone, Amber, Tiger's Eye

Rosemary, Cinnamon, Bay

VIRGO

Aug 23 | Sep 22

Innocent, Faithful, Practical, Anxious, Critical, Shy

Colors
Green, Brown

Rules the 6th House of
Health & Service

Earth

Peridot, Sapphire, Jasper

Fennel, Dill, Caraway

LIBRA

Sep 23 | Oct 22

Charming, Fair, Sincere, Restless, Objective, Indecisive

Colors
Blue, Pink

Rules the 7th House of
Partnership

Air

Lapis Lazuli, Opal, Tourmaline

Catnip, Thyme, Yarrow

SCORPIO

Oct 23 | Nov 21

Idealistic, Alert, Driven, Jealous, Vindictive, Clingy

Colors
Black, red

Rules the 8th House of
Death & Rebirth

Water

Obsidian, Garnet, Malachite

Basil, Patchouli, Ginger

SAGITTARIUS

Nov 22 | Dec 21

Optimistic, Versatile, Moral, Irresponsible, Tactless, Lazy

Colors
Purple, Bleu

Rules the 9th House of
Philosophy

Fire

Turquoise, Topaz, Amethyst

Sage, Clove, Nutmeg

CAPRICORN

Dec 22 | Jan 19

Steadfast, Organized, Cautious, Insecure, Detached, Uptight

Colors
Black, Brown

Rules the 10th House of
Career

Earth

Onyx, Garnet, Jet

Comfrey, Rosemary, Solomon's Seal

AQUARIUS

Jan 20 | Feb 18

Sociable, Inventive, Intelligent, Eccentric, Flighty, Detached

Colors
Blue, Silver

Rules the 11th House of
Friends

Air

Amethyst, Garnet, Aquamarine

Anise, Peppermint, Chamomile

PISCES

Feb 19 | Mar 20

Sympathetic, Mystical, Intuitive, Escapist, Unrealistic, Passive

Colors
Sea Green, Lavender

Rules the 12th House of
Spirit

Water

Amethyst, Aquamarine, Bloodstone

Lemon Balm, Sage, Thyme

ELEMENTS CORRESPONDENCES
Cheat Sheet

EARTH	AIR	FIRE	WATER
North	East	South	West

 Winter

 Spring

 Summer

 Autumn

Feminine
Stability
Harmony
Nurturing
Fertile
Practical
Supportive

Masculine
Action
Knowledge
Communication
Clarity
Intellect
Intention

Masculine
Energy
Passion
Sexuality
Power
Creativity
Inner strength

Feminine
Intuition
Emotions
Relationships
Fluidity
Healing
Cleansing

Taurus
Virgo
Capricorn

Gemini
Libra
Aquarius

Aries
Leo
Sagittarius

Cancer
Scorpio
Pisces

Moon
Venus
Saturn

Jupiter
Mercury
Moon

Sun
Mars

Moon
Neptune
Pluto

New
Moon

Waning
Moon

Full
Moon

Waning
Moon

Malachite
Jade
Peridot
Emerald
Black Obsidian
Hematite

Sapphire
Citrine
Smoky Quartz
Tourmaline
Amethyst
Rhodonite

Carnelian
Amber
Garnet
Sunstone
Fire Opal

Amethyst
Aquamarine
Beryl
Sodalite
Lapis Lazuli
Fluorite

TAROT
SAMPLE QUESTIONS

About Love

About Money

About Spirituality

About Health

About Relationship

About Career

1- What is the current state of my love life?
2- How can I attract more love into my life?
3- What lessons can I learn from my past relationships?
4- What qualities should I look for in a romantic partner?
5- How can I improve communication with my partner?
6- What obstacles are preventing me from finding love?
7- What steps can I take to heal from a past heartbreak?
8- What is my love language, and how can I express it effectively?
9- What changes do I need to make to create a fulfilling relationship?
10- How can I strengthen the bond with my current partner?
11- What does my subconscious mind want me to know about love?
12- What role does self-love play in attracting a healthy relationship?
13- What hidden aspects of myself may be affecting my love life?
14- What can I do to overcome trust issues in my relationships?
15- How can I release any fears or insecurities related to love?
16- What actions can I take to deepen intimacy with my partner?
17- How can I balance my personal goals with my relationship aspirations?
18- What do I need to forgive myself or others for in past relationships?
19- What patterns do I need to break to experience lasting love?
20- How can I set healthy boundaries in my relationships?
21- What does my intuition tell me about my current romantic situation?
22- How can I manifest the love I desire into my life?
23- What messages do the cards have regarding my soulmate?
24- How can I let go of attachment to a specific outcome in love?
25- What lessons am I meant to learn from my current relationship challenges?
26- How can I create more passion and excitement in my love life?
27- What unconscious beliefs do I hold about love that may be limiting me?
28- How can I cultivate gratitude for the love I already have in my life?
29- What areas of my life need more balance to support a healthy relationship?
30- How can I release any past regrets or resentments related to love?
31- What steps can I take to attract a loving and supportive partner?
32- How can I overcome feelings of loneliness or isolation in my love life?
33- What messages do my dreams hold about my romantic future?
34- How can I infuse more fun and playfulness into my relationships?
35- What does the future hold for my current relationship?
36- How can I maintain independence while still being in a committed relationship?
37- What do I need to let go of to make space for new love to enter my life?
38- How can I deepen my spiritual connection with my partner?
39- What aspects of myself do I need to work on to become a better partner?
40- How can I trust the timing of the universe when it comes to love?
41- What role does self-care play in nurturing my relationships?
42- How can I overcome any feelings of unworthiness in love?
43- What do I need to communicate more clearly to my partner?
44- How can I release any attachment to past romantic ideals that no longer serve me?
45- What qualities do I possess that make me a great partner?
46- How can I embrace vulnerability in my relationships?
47- What unconscious fears are holding me back from experiencing true love?
48- How can I let go of comparison and jealousy in my relationships?
49- What can I do to infuse more romance into my daily life?
50- How can I honor my own needs while still being supportive of my partner's?

50 QUESTIONS
Money

1- How can I use my financial resources to create a life of abundance and fulfillment?
2- What financial opportunities should I be aware of right now?
3- How can I improve my financial abundance and prosperity?
4- What lessons can I learn from past financial challenges?
5- What is blocking me from achieving my financial goals?
6- How can I attract more wealth and abundance into my life?
7- What steps can I take to increase my income?
8- What areas of my life need more financial discipline?
9- What investments or financial ventures should I consider?
10- How can I overcome any limiting beliefs about money?
11- What is my true relationship with money, and how can I improve it?
12- What actions can I take to manifest financial success?
13- What do I need to release to create more financial freedom?
14- How can I manage my finances more effectively?
15- What opportunities are available for me to grow my wealth?
16- How can I align my work with my financial goals?
17- What steps can I take to save more money and reduce expenses?
18- What do I need to learn about managing money wisely?
19- How can I attract abundance and prosperity into all areas of my life?
20- What financial skills or knowledge do I need to develop?
21- What resources or support do I need to achieve financial stability?
22- How can I overcome any fears or anxieties related to money?
23- What role does gratitude play in attracting wealth and abundance?
24- How can I use my talents and skills to generate more income?
25- What opportunities for financial growth are available to me in the near future?
26- How can I balance enjoying life with being financially responsible?
27- What do I need to let go of to create space for financial abundance?
28- How can I attract more opportunities for prosperity into my life?
29- What do I need to focus on to achieve long-term financial security?
30- How can I use my resources more wisely to build wealth?
31- What is the best approach for me to achieve my financial goals?
32- How can I overcome any self-sabotaging behaviors related to money?
33- What steps can I take to create multiple streams of income?
34- How can I use the law of attraction to manifest wealth and success?
35- What financial patterns or cycles do I need to break?
36- How can I make smarter financial decisions?
37- What do I need to know about my current financial path?
38- How can I use my money to make a positive impact in the world?
39- What do I need to do to attract financial abundance effortlessly?
40- How can I create a mindset of abundance and prosperity?
41- What do I need to release to overcome any financial obstacles?
42- How can I increase my confidence in managing money?
43- What steps can I take to build a stable financial foundation?
44- How can I attract more opportunities for wealth and success?
45- What financial opportunities are available to me that I may be overlooking?
46- How can I use my creativity to generate wealth?
47- What do I need to know about my financial future?
48- How can I overcome any resistance to receiving abundance?
49- What actions can I take to achieve financial freedom?
50- How can I use my financial resources to create a life of abundance and fulfillment?

1- What is my current spiritual path or journey?

2- What spiritual lessons am I meant to learn at this time?

3- How can I deepen my connection to the divine or higher power?

4- What practices or rituals can enhance my spiritual growth?

5- What is my soul's purpose in this lifetime?

6- How can I overcome any spiritual blocks or obstacles?

7- What signs or synchronicities should I pay attention to?

8- How can I cultivate more inner peace and serenity?

9- What spiritual gifts or abilities do I possess?

10- How can I align my actions with my spiritual values?

11- What do I need to release to experience spiritual liberation?

12- How can I connect more deeply with my intuition?

13- What messages does the universe have for me at this time?

14- How can I cultivate a sense of gratitude in my spiritual practice?

15- What practices can help me stay grounded and centered?

16- How can I integrate spirituality into my daily life?

17- What do I need to forgive myself or others for on a spiritual level?

18- How can I deepen my understanding of universal truths?

19- What spiritual teachings or philosophies resonate with me?

20- How can I trust the guidance of my inner wisdom?

21- What role does self-love play in my spiritual journey?

22- How can I connect with my spirit guides or guardian angels?

23- What past life experiences are influencing my spiritual path?

24- How can I release any fears or doubts about my spiritual journey?

25- What steps can I take to live in alignment with my higher self?

26- How can I embrace the concept of oneness with all beings?

27- What spiritual practices can help me cultivate compassion?

28- How can I surrender control and trust in the divine plan?

29- What lessons can I learn from nature and the natural world?

30- How can I tap into my inner wisdom and intuition more effectively?

31- What role does meditation play in my spiritual growth?

32- How can I let go of attachment to outcomes and embrace divine timing?

33- What past traumas do I need to heal on a spiritual level?

34- How can I honor and nurture my spiritual gifts and abilities?

35- What do I need to know about my soul's journey in this lifetime?

36- How can I find meaning and purpose in challenging situations?

37- What spiritual practices can help me navigate times of uncertainty?

38- How can I deepen my connection to the divine feminine or masculine?

39- What sacred symbols or archetypes are guiding me on my journey?

40- How can I cultivate more awareness and presence in my spiritual practice?

41- What do I need to release to experience spiritual transformation?

42- How can I connect with my ancestors or lineage for guidance?

43- What role does gratitude play in my spiritual evolution?

44- How can I integrate shadow work into my spiritual practice?

45- What do I need to know about my connection to the cosmos?

46- How can I cultivate more trust in the universe and divine timing?

47- What spiritual practices can help me navigate transitions and change?

48- How can I create a sacred space for my spiritual practice?

49- What messages are my dreams trying to convey to me?

50- How can I embrace the journey of self-discovery and spiritual growth?

1- What is the current state of my physical health?
2- What lifestyle changes can I make to improve my overall well-being?
3- How can I cultivate a healthier relationship with food?
4- What habits or behaviors may be impacting my health negatively?
5- What areas of my body need more attention and care?
6- What underlying emotional issues may be affecting my physical health?
7- How can I find balance between work, rest, and play for optimal health?
8- What do I need to know about any current health challenges I'm facing?
9- What preventive measures can I take to safeguard my health?
10- How can I boost my immune system naturally?
11- What forms of exercise or movement would benefit me the most?
12- What dietary changes can support my specific health goals?
13- How can I reduce stress and manage my emotions for better health?
14- What holistic practices or therapies would be beneficial for me?
15- What messages do my body's symptoms hold for me?
16- How can I listen to and honor my body's needs more effectively?
17- What energetic blockages may be contributing to my health issues?
18- What do I need to release to experience greater vitality and energy?
19- How can I cultivate a positive mindset for improved health?
20- What self-care practices can I incorporate into my daily routine?
21- What do I need to know about any chronic health conditions I'm dealing with?
22- How can I improve my sleep quality and overall restfulness?
23- What role does self-love play in my journey to better health?
24- How can I overcome any resistance to making healthier choices?
25- What alternative or complementary therapies may benefit me?
26- How can I tap into my body's natural healing abilities?
27- What do I need to let go of to experience greater physical wellness?
28- How can I foster a sense of gratitude for my body and its abilities?
29- What messages do my dreams hold regarding my health and well-being?
30- How can I create a supportive environment for my health goals?
31- What past traumas or experiences may be affecting my health?
32- How can I build a stronger connection between mind, body, and spirit?
33- What do I need to know about any potential health risks in my life?
34- How can I cultivate more resilience in the face of health challenges?
35- What steps can I take to improve my digestive health?
36- How can I release any fears or anxieties related to my health?
37- What affirmations or mantras can support my healing journey?
38- How can I better manage any chronic pain or discomfort I experience?
39- What do I need to learn about listening to my body's intuitive wisdom?
40- How can I find joy and pleasure in nourishing my body?
41- What do I need to know about my body's energy centers (chakras) and their balance?
42- How can I support my body's detoxification processes?
43- What nutritional supplements or herbs may benefit me?
44- How can I cultivate more patience and acceptance on my healing journey?
45- What role does forgiveness play in my journey to better health?
46- How can I create a sense of empowerment around my health choices?
47- What ancestral or familial health patterns do I need to be aware of?
48- How can I embrace a holistic approach to my health and well-being?
49- What steps can I take to prevent burnout and maintain balance in my life?
50- How can I celebrate and honor my body for its resilience and strength?

1- What is the current state of my relationship with my family members?

2- How can I improve communication with my siblings?

3- What do I need to know about my relationship with my parents?

4- How can I cultivate more harmony in my friendships?

5- What lessons can I learn from my closest friends?

6- How can I strengthen my bonds with my coworkers?

7- What do I need to know about my relationship with my boss or supervisor?

8- How can I navigate conflicts with my colleagues more effectively?

9- What do I need to release to experience greater connection with my peers?

10- How can I create healthier boundaries in my professional relationships?

11- What role do my mentors or advisors play in my life?

12- How can I attract more supportive mentors into my life?

13- What do I need to learn from my past relationships with authority figures?

14- How can I foster more collaboration and teamwork in my professional life?

15- What do I need to know about my relationship with my neighbors?

16- How can I cultivate a sense of community in my neighborhood?

17- What lessons can I learn from my interactions with acquaintances?

18- How can I be more present in my social interactions?

19- What do I need to release to experience more authentic connections?

20- How can I show more appreciation for the people in my life?

21- What do I need to know about my relationship with my pets?

22- How can I deepen my bond with my animal companions?

23- What messages do my pets have for me at this time?

24- How can I be a better caregiver to my pets?

25- What do I need to release to experience more joy and fulfillment in my relationships?

26- How can I support my loved ones during challenging times?

27- What do I need to know about my relationship with my spiritual community?

28- How can I contribute positively to my spiritual community?

29- What do I need to learn from my interactions with spiritual leaders or teachers?

30- How can I cultivate more compassion and understanding in my relationships?

31- What do I need to release to experience more peace and harmony in my relationships?

32- How can I be a better listener in my interactions with others?

33- What do I need to know about my relationship with social media and technology?

34- How can I use social media and technology to deepen my connections?

35- What do I need to release to experience healthier boundaries with technology?

36- How can I cultivate more authenticity in my online relationships?

37- What do I need to learn from my experiences with online communities?

38- How can I navigate online conflicts or misunderstandings with grace?

39- What do I need to know about my relationship with money and finances?

40- How can I cultivate a healthier attitude towards wealth and abundance?

41- What do I need to release to experience more abundance in my life?

42- How can I improve my financial communication with my loved ones?

43- What do I need to learn from past financial conflicts with family or friends?

44- How can I support my loved ones in their financial goals and aspirations?

45- What do I need to know about my relationship with my physical environment?

46- How can I create a more nurturing and supportive living space?

47- What messages does my home environment have for me at this time?

48- How can I foster more harmony and balance in my home life?

49- What do I need to release to create a more peaceful and loving home environment?

50- How can I express more gratitude for the relationships in my life?

50 QUESTIONS
Career

1- What is the current state of my career path?
2- What opportunities are available to me in my career right now?
3- How can I advance in my current job or profession?
4- What do I need to know about my career goals and aspirations?
5- What steps can I take to find greater fulfillment in my work?
6- What skills or talents should I focus on developing for career success?
7- What obstacles may be hindering my career progress?
8- How can I overcome any challenges or setbacks in my career?
9- What do I need to release to experience more abundance in my career?
10- How can I align my career with my passions and interests?
11- What do I need to learn from past career experiences or mistakes?
12- What opportunities for growth and expansion are on the horizon in my career?
13- How can I improve my professional relationships with colleagues and superiors?
14- What do I need to know about my current job or workplace environment?
15- How can I find more meaning and purpose in my career path?
16- What do I need to do to increase my earning potential in my career?
17- How can I navigate career transitions or changes with confidence?
18- What do I need to release to overcome any fears or doubts about my career?
19- How can I create a better work-life balance in my career?
20- What do I need to know about my unique strengths and talents in the workplace?
21- What role does networking play in advancing my career?
22- How can I improve my professional reputation and credibility?
23- What steps can I take to stand out and be recognized in my field?
24- What do I need to learn from successful mentors or role models in my industry?
25- How can I make a positive impact and contribute meaningfully in my career?
26- What do I need to release to experience greater success and fulfillment in my career?
27- How can I leverage my creativity to enhance my career prospects?
28- What opportunities for leadership or entrepreneurship are available to me?
29- How can I overcome any self-limiting beliefs or imposter syndrome in my career?
30- What do I need to know about my career path in the long term?
31- How can I create a clear and actionable career plan?
32- What do I need to learn from any past career failures or setbacks?
33- How can I enhance my professional skills and qualifications?
34- What steps can I take to find a career that aligns with my values and principles?
35- How can I cultivate more confidence and assertiveness in my career?
36- What do I need to release to experience more joy and fulfillment in my career?
37- How can I navigate office politics or workplace conflicts gracefully?
38- What role does self-care play in achieving success and balance in my career?
39- How can I create a supportive network of mentors and allies in my industry?
40- What do I need to know about any potential career opportunities or changes on the horizon?
41- How can I use setbacks or challenges as opportunities for growth in my career?
42- What steps can I take to position myself as an expert or authority in my field?
43- How can I find more satisfaction and fulfillment in my current job role?
44- What do I need to release to experience greater abundance and prosperity in my career?
45- How can I overcome any feelings of stagnation or lack of progress in my career?
46- What do I need to know about the impact of my career choices on my overall well-being?
47- How can I cultivate a positive and optimistic mindset in my career endeavors?
48- What steps can I take to create a career path that reflects my true passions and interests?
49- How can I find more balance between pursuing my career goals and nurturing other aspects of my life?
50- What do I need to do to create a career that brings me joy, fulfillment, and abundance?

Major
TAROT CARDS

The Fool	Justice
The Magician	The Hanged Man
The High Priestess	Death
The Empress	Temperance
The Emperor	The Devil
The Hierophant	The Tower
The Lovers	The Star
The Chariot	The Moon
Strength	The Sun
The Hermit	Judgement
Wheel of Fortune	The World

0 | ZERO
New Beginnings, freedom.

THE FOOL.

The Fool

"COSMIC BEGINNINGS AND INFINITE POSSIBILITIES"
With a carefree figure on the brink of stepping off a cliff,
it represents the boundless journey of the soul.

Uriel
Archangel

Fire
Element

Crown
Chakras

Spiritual
Domain

Uranus
Planet

Optimism, energy, intellect.
YELLOW

Purity, innocence, clarity.
WHITE

Passion, action, courage.
RED

Intuition, openness to possibilities, spiritual connection.
BLUE

MOUNTAINS:
Overcoming obstacles, challenges.

CLIFF EDGE:
Bold leaps of faith.

TUNIC:
Simple, carefree attire.

RED FEATHER:
Symbol of courage, vitality.

WHITE DOG:
Faithful companionship, innocence.

WHITE FLOWER:
Purity, new beginnings.

BAG:
Carrying life's potential.

GENERAL
▲ New beginnings, innocence, faith, adventure.

▼ Recklessness, naivety, lack of direction.

LOVE
▲ New beginnings in love, open-mindedness, taking a leap of faith.

▼ Recklessness in love, rushing into relations, naive expectations.

MONEY
▲ New beginnings, fresh ideas, exploring investments.

▼ Recklessness, impulsive spending, lack of planning.

CAREER
▲ New beginnings, exploring options, taking risks, entrepreneurial ventures.

▼ Lack of direction, impulsiveness, careless career choices, neglecting responsibilities.

HEALTH-WELLBEING
▲ New beginnings, openness to alternative approaches, exploring holistic treatments.

▼ Recklessness, ignoring symptoms, lack of self-care.

SPIRITUALITY
▲ Spiritual trust, innocence, new journeys.

▼ Lack of faith, missteps, spiritual recklessness.

1 | ONE
Manifestation, power, action.

THE MAGICIAN.

HANDS AND WAND:
Commanding power, manifestation.

INFINITY SYMBOL:
Endless possibilities, mastery.

SERPENT BELT:
Transformation, ancient wisdom.

RED GOWN:
Willpower, creative energy.

WHITE ROBE:
Purity, spiritual connection.

FLOWERS:
Blooming potential, growth.

The Magician

"MANIFESTATION AND PERSONAL POWER"
The Magician, with one hand pointing to the heavens and the other to the earth, channels the energies of the cosmos.

Raphael	**Air**	**Third Eye**	**Mental**	**Mercury**
Archangel	*Element*	*Chakras*	*Domain*	*Planet*

YELLOW	RED	WHITE	BROWN
Intellect, communication, creativity.	Willpower, energy, determination.	Spiritual purity, clarity, truth.	Stability, earthiness, reliability.

GENERAL
▲ Manifestation, creativity, willpower, action.

▼ Manipulation, trickery, lack of focus.

LOVE
▲ Manifesting a desired relationship, using creativity to attract love, taking action.

▼ Manipulation in relationships, trickery, difficulty attracting love.

MONEY
▲ Manifestation, resourcefulness, attracting abundance.

▼ Lack of focus, manipulation, unrealistic expectations.

CAREER
▲ Manifestation, resourcefulness, turning ideas into reality, skilled communication.

▼ Manipulation, missed opportunities, lack of focus, neglecting self-promotion.

HEALTH-WELLBEING
▲ Manifestation, using visualization for healing, taking action.

▼ Lack of focus, manipulation, unrealistic expectations of recovery.

SPIRITUALITY
▲ Manifestation, spiritual power, personal alchemy.

▼ Manipulation, spiritual imbalance, egoism.

2 | TWO
Intuition, mystery, knowledge.

THE HIGH PRIESTESS

The High Priestess

"INTUITION AND MYSTERY"
Seated between the pillars of knowledge and intuition,
The High Priestess guards esoteric wisdom.

Gabriel
Archangel

Water
Element

Crown
Chakras

Spiritual
Domain

Moon
Planet

Intuition, mystery, depth.	Purity, spiritual connection, truth.
BLUE	**WHITE**
Mystery, intuition, protection, hidden knowledge.	Intellect, wisdom, clarity guidance.
BLACK	**YELLOW**

TORA SCROLL:
Ancient wisdom, sacred knowledge.

MOON CROWN:
Intuition, divine connection.

WHITE CROSS:
Spiritual balance, duality.

VEIL:
Hidden mysteries, intuition.

BLACK AND WHITE PILLAR:
Dual nature, balance.

BLUE ROBE:
Mystical depth, serenity.

B AND J:
Boaz and Jachin.

GENERAL
▲ Intuition, wisdom, knowledge, secrets.

▼ Doubt, confusion, lack of access to intuition.

LOVE
▲ Intuition guiding your love life, trusting your gut, hidden feelings.

▼ Confusion about love, difficulty connecting with intuition, hidden agendas.

MONEY
▲ Intuition, hidden potential, seeking financial knowledge.

▼ Confusion, indecisiveness, fear of taking action.

CAREER
▲ Inner wisdom, intuition guiding career decisions, hidden potential, untapped skills.

▼ Stagnation, indecisiveness, fear of success, lacking confidence in abilities.

HEALTH-WELLBEING
▲ Intuition, listening to your body, seeking internal wisdom.

▼ Confusion, neglecting intuition, ignoring signs of imbalance.

SPIRITUALITY
▲ Intuition, mysticism, inner wisdom.

▼ Ignoring intuition, spiritual blockage, hidden secrets.

3 | THREE
Fertility, abundance, nurture.

THE EMPRESS.

The Empress

"NURTURING AND ABUNDANCE"
Seated amidst lush nature,
The Empress symbolizes fertility and growth.

Anael
Archangel

Earth
Element

Sacral
Chakras

Physical
Domain

Venus
Planet

Fertility, growth, nature. **GREEN**	Passion, vitality, fertility, motherhood **RED**	Purity, innocence. **WHITE**	Abundance, prosperity, creativity, inspiration. **YELLOW**

CROWN:
Regal authority, abundance.

WREATH:
Fertility, life's cycles.

SCEPTER:
Nurturing power, creation.

GOWN:
Maternal, earthly elegance.

PEARL NECKLACE:
Elegance, wisdom, abundance.

WATERFALL:
Flowing emotions, abundance.

WHEAT:
Harvest, abundance, sustenance.

GENERAL
▲ Nurturing, abundance, fertility, creativity.

▼ Smothering, possessiveness, creative block.

LOVE
▲ Nurturing love, fertility, abundance in relationships, creative partnerships.

▼ Smothering in love, possessiveness, difficulty establishing independence.

MONEY
▲ Growth, abundance, security, long-term investments.

▼ Overindulgence, wastefulness, dependence on others.

CAREER
▲ Growth, abundance, nurturing projects, fostering creativity, attracting resources.

▼ Stagnation, lack of progress, overindulgence in comfort zone, dependence on others.

HEALTH-WELLBEING
▲ Nurturing, self-care, healthy habits, abundance of energy.

▼ Overindulgence, unhealthy lifestyle choices, dependence on others.

SPIRITUALITY
▲ Nurturing spirit, creativity, spiritual fertility.

▼ Imbalance, spiritual stagnation, dependency.

4 | FOUR
Authority, structure, control.

THE EMPEROR.

The Emperor

"AUTHORITY AND STRUCTURE"
Seated on a throne adorned with ram's heads,
The Emperor represents leadership and order.

Camael	Earth	Plexus	Physical	Aries
Archangel	*Element*	*Chakras*	*Domain*	*Zodiac*

Power, passion, action.	Creativity, innovation, balancing authority.	Intellect, clarity, confidence and power.	Authority, stability, wisdom, Knowledge.
RED	**ORANGE**	**YELLOW**	**BLUE**

RAMS HEADS:
Leadership, strength, power.

CROWN:
Sovereignty, authority, rule.

ARMOR:
Protective strength, authority.

ANKH CROSS:
Life, vitality, divine authority.

MOUNTAINS:
Stability, solid foundation.

RIVER:
Flow of authority, control.

GENERAL
▲ Structure, stability, authority, leadership.

▼ Rigidity, control, dominance.

LOVE
▲ Stable and secure relationships, commitment, leadership in love.

▼ Rigidity in relationships, controlling behavior, difficulty compromising.

MONEY
▲ Stability, structure, budgeting, planning for the future.

▼ Rigidity, inflexibility, fear of taking risks.

CAREER
▲ Structure, organization, stability, leadership, taking control of career path.

▼ Rigidity, inflexibility, controlling behavior, micromanagement.

HEALTH-WELLBEING
▲ Stability, structure, routine, discipline in self-care.

▼ Rigidity, inflexibility, resisting change, neglecting emotional well-being.

SPIRITUALITY
▲ Spiritual order, structure, authority.

▼ Tyranny, rigidity, spiritual control.

5 | FIVE
Tradition, wisdom, guidance.

THE HIEROPHANT

The Hierophant

"TRADITION AND SPIRITUAL GUIDANCE"
Seated between two acolytes,
The Hierophant imparts wisdom and spiritual teachings.

Anael	**Earth**	**Throat**	**Spiritual**	**Taurus**
Archangel	*Element*	*Chakras*	*Domain*	*Zodiac*

RED	WHITE	GREY	YELLOW
Spiritual passion, sacred rituals.	Purity, spirituality, truth.	Neutrality, mystery, wisdom.	Enlightenment, intellect, positivity.

CROWN:
Spiritual authority, wisdom.

BLUE SCARF:
Spiritual purity, devotion.

SCEPTER:
Divine guidance, leadership.

BENEDICTION:
Blessings, spiritual grace.

CROSSED KEYS:
Knowledge, access to mysteries.

MONKS:
Spiritual community, wisdom.

PILLARS:
Duality, divine connection.

GENERAL
▲ Tradition, conformity, teaching, guidance.

▼ Dogmatism, judgment, blind faith.

LOVE
▲ Traditional values in love, seeking approval, commitment ceremonies.

▼ Dogmatism in relationships, getting stuck in outdated views, fear of change.

MONEY
▲ Traditional financial values, seeking advice from experts.

▼ Dogmatism, outdated practices, following others blindly.

CAREER
▲ Traditional paths, established institutions, seeking guidance, mentors.

▼ Blind trust, outdated practices, following the crowd, neglecting innovation.

HEALTH-WELLBEING
▲ Traditional treatments, seeking professional guidance, following medical advice.

▼ Dogmatism, clinging to outdated methods, ignoring alternative approaches.

SPIRITUALITY
▲ Spiritual tradition, guidance, religious practices.

▼ Rebellion, nonconformity, questioning tradition.

6 | SIX
Love, union, choices.

THE LOVERS.

ANGEL RAPHAEL:
Healing guidance, divine support.

SUN:
Ilumination, positive energy.

COUPLE:
Harmony, choices, relationships.

TREES:
Growth, life's journey.

APPLE:
Temptation, choices, awareness.

SNAKE:
Transformation, duality, renewal.

MOUNTAIN:
Overcoming challenges, elevation.

The Lovers

"LOVE AND UNION"
A couple beneath an angel,
The Lovers symbolize love, choices, and spiritual connection.

| **Raphael** *Archangel* | **Air** *Element* | **Heart** *Chakras* | **Emotional** *Domain* | **Gemini** *Zodiac* |

| Intellectual connection, shared values. | Passionate love, intense emotions, desires. | Tender affection, emotional intimacy, empathy. | Connection, communication, serenity. |
| YELLOW | RED | PINK | BLUE |

GENERAL

▲ Choice, relationships, balance, harmony.

▼ Confusion, indecision, imbalance, disharmony.

LOVE

▲ Making a choice in love, finding balance and harmony, soul connections.

▼ Difficulty choosing, indecisiveness, imbalance in relationships.

MONEY

▲ Balancing income and expenses, making wise choices, partnerships.

▼ Indecision, unclear financial goals, conflicting advice.

CAREER

▲ Collaboration, balance, partnerships, making career choices, finding mentors.

▼ Disconnection, conflict, imbalance, indecisiveness in collaboration, unhealthy partnerships.

HEALTH-WELLBEING

▲ Balance, finding the right approach, integrating different viewpoints.

▼ Indecision, conflicting advice, confusion about treatment options.

SPIRITUALITY

▲ Soul connection, divine love, spiritual union.

▼ Disharmony, conflicting values, spiritual distance.

7 | SEVEN
Willpower, triumph, drive.

THE CHARIOT.

The Chariot

"DETERMINATION AND CONTROL"
A charioteer steering two sphinxes,
The Chariot symbolizes triumph through determination.

Gabriel *Archangel*   **Water** *Element*   **Plexus** *Chakras*   **Mental** *Domain*   **Cancer** *Zodiac*

BLACK	WHITE	YELLOW	BLUE
Strength, mystery, control.	Balance, purity, clarity.	Intellectual strength, optimism, enlightenment.	Focus, control, intuition.

MOON SIGN:
Subconscious guidance.

STAR CROWN:
Celestial alignment.

AMULET:
Spiritual protection.

WAND:
Willpower and direction.

ANGEL WINGS:
Spiritual elevation.

TOWN, MOAT:
Overcoming challenges.

GENERAL
▲ Control, direction, willpower, determination.

▼ Lack of control, impulsiveness, recklessness.

LOVE
▲ Taking control of your love life, pursuing desires, overcoming obstacles.

▼ Recklessness in love, rushing into things, impulsive decisions.

MONEY
▲ Perseverance, overcoming obstacles, taking control of finances.

▼ Impulsiveness, lack of direction, taking unnecessary risks..

CAREER
▲ Willpower, determination, overcoming obstacles, achieving career goals.

▼ Lack of control, procrastination, direction lessness, giving up easily.

HEALTH-WELLBEING
▲ Perseverance, overcoming challenges, taking control of your health.

▼ Impulsiveness, lack of direction, taking unnecessary risks.

SPIRITUALITY
▲ Spiritual victory, determination, control.

▼ Spiritual conflict, lack of direction, inner turmoil.

8 | EIGHT
Courage, patience, inner strength.

Strength

"INNER STRENGTH AND COURAGE"
Depicting a figure gently taming a lion,
Strength symbolizes compassion and inner power.

Michael
Archangel

Fire
Element

Heart
Chakras

Emotional
Domain

Leo
Zodiac

GREY — Wisdom, tranquility, resilience, maturity.

WHITE — Purity, spiritual strength, divine guidance.

ORANGE — Passion, vitality, energetic.

GREEN — Kindness, empathy, harmony.

WOMAN:
Inner strength, grace.

LION:
Taming primal instincts.

WHITE DRESS:
Purity, authenticity.

INFINITY SIGN:
Enduring spiritual strength.

BLUE MOUNTAIN:
Stability, overcoming challenges.

FLOWER BELT:
Harmony of strength, beauty.

GENERAL
▲ Gentle persuasion, inner strength, compassion.

▼ Domination, control, aggression.

LOVE
▲ Gentle persuasion in relationships, compassion, overcoming challenges.

▼ Domination in love, manipulation, aggressiveness.

MONEY
▲ Negotiation, finding leverage, fair deals.

▼ Aggression, domination, manipulative financial practices.

CAREER
▲ Inner strength, overcoming challenges, facing adversity, standing up for yourself.

▼ Timidity, self-doubt, fear of conflict, being taken advantage of.

HEALTH-WELLBEING
▲ Gentle self-compassion, inner strength, facing fears.

▼ Aggression, self-criticism, resistance to healing.

SPIRITUALITY
▲ Inner strength, courage, spiritual endurance.

▼ Weakness, self-doubt, spiritual vulnerability.

9 | NINE
Solitude, insight, enlightenment.

THE HERMIT.

The Hermit

"SOUL SEARCHING AND REFLECTION"
Depicting a wise figure with a lantern, The Hermit symbolizes seeking inner truth.

Raphael
Archangel

Earth
Element

Third Eye
Chakras

Spiritual
Domain

Capricorn
Zodiac

GREY	BLUE	YELLOW	BROWN
Wisdom, neutrality, solitude.	Introspection, spirituality, reflection.	Inner light, wisdom, enlightenment	Earthiness, stability, simplicity.

OLD MAN:
Wisdom, experience.

GRAY CLOAK:
Concealed wisdom, introspection.

LAMP:
Inner guidance, enlightenment.

STAR:
Inspiration, hope, higher guidance.

GOLD WAND:
Spiritual authority, divine knowledge.

SNOW:
Purity, stillness in solitude.

MOUNTAIN TOP:
Ascension through introspection.

GENERAL
▲ Introspection, solitude, seeking wisdom, meditation.

▼ Isolation, withdrawal, loneliness.

LOVE
▲ Seeking solitude to reflect on love, introspection, self-discovery.

▼ Isolation in love, withdrawing from relationships, loneliness.

MONEY
▲ Seeking financial independence, introspection, self-reliance.

▼ Isolation, neglecting responsibilities, fear of sharing.

CAREER
▲ Introspection, reflection, seeking knowledge, honing skills, sabbatical or solo ventures.

▼ Isolation, withdrawal, fear of connection, neglecting networking, missing opportunities.

HEALTH-WELLBEING
▲ Introspection, seeking solitude for reflection, self-healing practices.

▼ Isolation, neglecting social support, difficulty seeking help.

SPIRITUALITY
▲ Spiritual insight, solitude, seeking truth.

▼ Isolation, loneliness, avoidance.

10 | TEN
Destiny, change, cycles.

WHEEL of FORTUNE.

Wheel of Fortune

"DESTINY AND CYCLES"
Depicting a wheel with symbolic figures,
it symbolizes the cyclical nature of life.

Sachiel
Archangel

Fire
Element

Plexus
Chakras

Spiritual
Domain

Jupiter
Planet

Neutrality, balance, transition, transformation.	Growth, fertility, abundance.	Action, fate, energy.	Cycles, optimism, enlightenment.
GREY	**ORANGE**	**RED**	**YELLOW**

ROTA:
Latin for rotation, cyclical nature.

ALCHEMY SYMBOLS:
Representing Earth, Water, Air, Fire – elemental balance.

ANGEL:
Divine intervention, celestial influence.

EAGLE:
Air element, perception, vision.

BULL:
Earth element, stability, strength.

LION:
Fire element, passion, courage.

SNAKE:
Water element, intuition, fluidity.

GENERAL

▲ Change, cycles, fate, karma.

▼ Unexpected change, instability, stagnation.

LOVE

▲ Unexpected changes in love, adapting to new situations, embracing fate.

▼ Instability in relationships, fear of change, clinging to the past.

MONEY

▲ Unexpected changes, adapting to financial fluctuations.

▼ Instability, fear of change, clinging to the past.

CAREER

▲ Unexpected change, career pivots, adapting to new opportunities.

▼ Resistance to change, clinging to the past, clinging to unstable situations.

HEALTH-WELLBEING

▲ Unexpected changes, adapting to new diagnoses, embracing healing journeys.

▼ Instability, fear of change, clinging to unhealthy patterns.

SPIRITUALITY

▲ Spiritual destiny, divine timing, change.

▼ Bad luck, resistance, spiritual stagnation.

11 | ELEVEN
Fairness, truth, balance.

JUSTICE .

Justice
"FAIRNESS AND BALANCE"

Depicting a figure holding scales,
Justice symbolizes impartiality and balance.

Anael
Archangel

Air
Element

Throat
Chakras

Mental
Domain

Libra
Zodiac

Justice, action, authority.	Spiritual balance, wisdom.	Clarity, rationality, objectivity.	Communication, fairness, harmony, balance.
RED	**PURPLE**	**YELLOW**	**BLUE**

SWORD:
Discernment, truth, justice.

SCALES:
Balance, impartial judgment.

PILLARS:
Ethical foundation, legal structure.

VEIL:
Hidden truths, transparency.

CROWN:
Authority, divine influence.

WHITE SHOE:
Purity in justice.

BROOCH:
Nuanced understanding of justice.

GENERAL
▲ Fairness, balance, accountability, karma.

▼ Dishonesty, unfairness, lack of accountability.

LOVE
▲ Fairness and honesty in relationships, accountability, seeking balance.

▼ Dishonesty in love, unfair treatment, difficulty letting go of grudges.

MONEY
▲ Fairness, ethical investments, accountability.

▼ Dishonesty, imbalance, unfair treatment.

CAREER
▲ Fairness, ethics, integrity, balancing work and personal life, accountability.

▼ Unfairness, ignoring ethical concerns, neglecting work-life balance, taking advantage of others.

HEALTH-WELLBEING
▲ Fairness, seeking ethical treatment, advocating for your health needs.

▼ Dishonesty, imbalance, unequal access to care.

SPIRITUALITY
▲ Spiritual balance, karma, divine justice.

▼ Imbalance, injustice, spiritual unfairness.

12 | TWELVE
Suspension, sacrifice, perspective.

THE HANGED MAN.

The Hanged Man

"SURRENDER AND PERSPECTIVE SHIFTS"
Depicting a figure suspended upside-down,
it symbolizes sacrifice and a change in perspective.

Asariel
Archangel

Water
Element

Crown
Chakras

Spiritual
Domain

Neptune
Planet

Surrender, intuition.

BLUE

Illumination, wisdom, enlightenment.

YELLOW

Detachment, neutrality, wisdom.

GREY

Acceptance, growth, balance.

GREEN

TREE:
Stability, life, growth.

CROSSED LEGS:
Balanced pause, reflection.

TAU CROSS:
Sacrifice, rebirth.

HALO:
Spiritual enlightenment,
divine connection.

RIGHT FOOT:
Willing surrender, voluntary
sacrifice.

GENERAL

▲ Surrender, new perspective, sacrifice, acceptance.

▼ Stagnation, resistance to change, procrastination.

LOVE

▲ Letting go of unhealthy attachments, sacrificing for love, new perspectives.

▼ Stagnation in relationships, avoiding commitment, difficulty letting go.

MONEY

▲ Letting go of unhealthy attachments, sacrifice for future benefits.

▼ Stagnation, resistance to change, fear of letting go.

CAREER

▲ New perspectives, letting go of outdated ideas, sacrifice for long-term goals.

▼ Stagnation, indecisiveness, fear of change, clinging to the past.

HEALTH-WELLBEING

▲ Letting go of control, surrendering to the healing process, new perspectives.

▼ Stagnation, resistance to change, fear of letting go.

SPIRITUALITY

▲ Spiritual surrender, new perspectives, letting go.

▼ Resistance, spiritual stagnation, fear of change.

13 | THIRTEEN
Transformation, endings, beginnings.

Death

"TRANSFORMATION AND RENEWAL"
Depicting the skeletal figure of Death,
it symbolizes the natural cycle of transformation and rebirth.

Azrael
Archangel

Water
Element

Root
Chakras

Emotional
Domain

Scorpio
Zodiac

BLACK
Transformation, endings, rebirth.

WHITE
Purity, liberation, transition.

RED
Renewal, life force, transformation.

GREY
Wisdom, detachment.

GRIM REAPER:
Transformation, rebirth.

HORSE:
End of a journey.

WHITE ROSE BANNER:
Purity, new beginnings.

RED FEATHER:
Vitality, life force.

BISHOP:
Spiritual transition.

KING:
Universality of death.

TOWERS:
Crumbling structures, change.

GENERAL
▲ Transformation, endings and beginnings, change.

▼ Resistance to change, fear of endings, stagnation.

LOVE
▲ Transformation in love, endings and new beginnings.

▼ Fear of change and endings, clinging to the past, resistance to transformation.

MONEY
▲ Transformation, endings and new financial beginnings, embracing change.

▼ Resistance to change, fear of loss, clinging to outdated strategies.

CAREER
▲ Transformation, reinvention, ending unfulfilling aspects of career, change in direction.

▼ Fear of change, resistance to transformation, clinging to dying projects.

HEALTH-WELLBEING
▲ Transformation, endings and new beginnings, releasing unhealthy habits.

▼ Resistance to change, fear of death, clinging to the past.

SPIRITUALITY
▲ Spiritual transformation, rebirth, endings.

▼ Resistance to change, clinging to past, stagnation.

14 | FOURTEEN
Balance, harmony, moderation.

Temperance

"HARMONY AND BALANCE"
Depicting an angel blending two cups, it symbolizes the alchemical process of combining opposing forces.

Sachiel
Archangel

Fire
Element

Throat
Chakras

Spiritual
Domain

Sagittarius
Zodiac

Balance, healing, harmony.
BLUE

Purity, innocence, and clarity.
WHITE

Transformation, divine connection.
PURPLE

Integration, wisdom, patience.
YELLOW

ANGEL:
Divine guidance, harmony.

GOLDEN DISK:
Vitality, enlightenment.

SQUARE:
Stability, balanced foundation.

CUPS:
Emotional blending, spiritual insight.

WATER:
Flow of emotions, intuitive connection.

PATH:
Balanced journey, moderation.

IRISES:
Spiritual insight, harmonious blossoming.

GENERAL
▲ Balance, moderation, integration, patience.

▼ Imbalance, extremes, impatience.

LOVE
▲ Finding balance in relationships, compromise, patience, moderation.

▼ Imbalance in love, extremes, rushing things, impatience.

MONEY
▲ Balance, moderation, responsible spending, budgeting.

▼ Imbalance, extremes, impulsive spending.

CAREER
▲ Balance, moderation, finding the middle ground, work-life harmony.

▼ Imbalance, extremes, burnout, neglecting important aspects of career or personal life.

HEALTH-WELLBEING
▲ Balance, moderation, mindful eating, integrating different healing methods.

▼ Imbalance, extremes, neglecting self-care, addictive behaviors.

SPIRITUALITY
▲ Spiritual balance, harmony, moderation.

▼ Imbalance, extremes, spiritual turmoil.

15 | FIFTEEN
Bondage, materialism, temptation.

THE DEVIL .

The Devil

"TEMPTATION AND MATERIALISM"
Depicting a demonic figure,
it symbolizes the allure of materialism and the bondage of desires.

Cassiel
Archangel

Earth
Element

Root
Chakras

Physical
Domain

Capricorn
Zodiac

Materialism, ignorance, attachment. **BLACK**	Desire, passion, temptation **RED**	Temptation, desires, bondage. **BROWN**	Earthly pleasures, sensuality, materialism **GREEN**

BAT WINGS:
Deceptive allure.

HORNS:
Corrupting influence.

DONKEY EARS:
Stubborn refusal.

INVERTED PENTACLES:
Material perversion.

MAN AND WOMAN:
Bondage to desires.

TAILS:
Passionate entanglement.

CHAINS:
Self-imposed bondage.

GENERAL
▲ Temptation, illusion, materialism, addiction.

▼ Freedom from illusion, overcoming temptation.

LOVE
▲ Temptation in relationships, hidden desires, unhealthy attachments.

▼ Facing your shadows, overcoming temptation, breaking free from negativity.

MONEY
▲ Temptation, hidden costs, unhealthy financial attachments.

▼ Overcoming temptation, facing financial realities, identifying risks.

CAREER
▲ Temptation, materialism, burnout, unhealthy work-life balance, hidden motivations.

▼ Overcoming negativity, finding purpose, setting boundaries, liberation from unhealthy work conditions.

HEALTH-WELLBEING
▲ Temptation, unhealthy habits, facing self-destructive patterns.

▼ Overcoming temptation, addressing hidden issues, seeking support.

SPIRITUALITY
▲ Materialism, spiritual bondage, temptation.

▼ Liberation, freedom, breaking chains.

16 | SIXTEEN
Upheaval, revelation, sudden change.

THE TOWER.

The Tower

"DESTRUCTION AND REVELATION"
Depicting a tower struck by lightning,
it symbolizes sudden upheaval and a revelation of truth.

Camael	**Fire**	**Crown**	**Physical**	**Mars**
Archangel	*Element*	*Chakras*	*Domain*	*Planet*

RED	**BLACK**	**GREY**	**YELLOW**
Destruction, transformation, renewal	Mystery, unknown, hidden meanings.	Chaos, sudden change, transformation.	Change, illumination, awakening.

TOWER:
False security, upheaval.

THREE WINDOWS:
Varied perspectives.

FALLING MAN AND WOMAN:
Sudden collapse of illusions.

LIGHTNING:
Divine revelation, truth.

YODS:
Transformative energy, renewal.

CROWN:
Dismantling false authority.

GENERAL
▲ Sudden change, disruption, upheaval, chaos.

▼ Personal transformation, release from limitations.

LOVE
▲ Sudden changes in love, disruptions, upheaval, unexpected revelations.

▼ Personal transformation in love, releasing limitations, finding strength in challenges.

MONEY
▲ Sudden disruptions, unexpected losses, change.

▼ Personal transformation, releasing limitations, learning from setbacks.

CAREER
▲ Sudden change, disruption, unexpected challenges, career upheaval.

▼ Resilience, overcoming adversity, personal growth, finding new opportunities.

HEALTH-WELLBEING
▲ Sudden changes, unexpected diagnoses, facing health challenges.

▼ Personal transformation, releasing limitations, finding strength in adversity.

SPIRITUALITY
▲ Spiritual awakening, radical change, revelation.

▼ Resistance, avoiding change, fear of upheaval.

17 | SEVENTEEN
Hope, inspiration, serenity

THE STAR.

The Star
"HOPE AND INSPIRATION"

Depicting a woman pouring water into a pool,
it symbolizes hope, inspiration, and spiritual insight.

Uriel
Archangel

Air
Element

Crown
Chakras

Spiritual
Domain

Aquarius
Zodiac

 Hope, inspiration, spiritual guidance.
BLUE

Purity, healing, divine connection.
WHITE

 Transformation, divine insight.
PURPLE

Hope, healing, growth, balance, harmony.
GREEN

MAIDEN:
Purity, renewal.

STARS:
Cosmic guidance, inspiration.

JUGS:
Balance of conscious and unconscious.

TREE:
Growth, interconnectedness.

BIRD:
Freedom, spiritual awakening.

MOUNTAIN:
Stability, endurance.

POOL:
Subconscious reflection, renewal.

GENERAL
▲ Hope, renewal, faith, inspiration.

▼ Disillusionment, hopelessness, loss of faith.

LOVE
▲ Hope and renewal in love, maintaining faith, following dreams.

▼ Disillusionment in love, loss of hope, cynicism.

MONEY
▲ Hope, renewal, maintaining faith, positive outlook.

▼ Disillusionment, cynicism, loss of hope.

CAREER
▲ Hope, inspiration, renewal, faith in your abilities, long-term vision.

▼ Disillusionment, lack of direction, pessimism, giving up on dreams.

HEALTH-WELLBEING
▲ Hope, renewal, maintaining faith, positive outlook.

▼ Disillusionment, cynicism, loss of hope.

SPIRITUALITY
▲ Hope, spiritual healing, inspiration.

▼ Loss of faith, despair, spiritual doubts.

18 | EIGHTEEN
Illusion, subconscious, mystery.

THE MOON.

The Moon

"ILLUSIONS AND INTUITION"
Depicting two towers, a path, and a crayfish emerging from the water,
it symbolizes the journey through illusions and intuition.

Sachiel *Archangel*   **Water** *Element*   **Third Eye** *Chakras*   **Emotional** *Domain*   **Moon** *Planet*

Intuition, mystery, subconscious.
BLUE

Illumination, intuition, clarity.
YELLOW

Reflective, intuitive, feminine energy.
SILVER

Trust instincts and tap into subconscious knowledge.
PURPLE

MOON:
Unconscious mind, mystery.

MOON-RAYS:
Mysterious illumination.

MOON-FACE:
Cyclical emotions.

CRAYFISH:
Emerging instincts.

DOG AND WOLF:
Dual nature.

PILLARS:
Gateway to the unknown.

BLUE LAND:
Realm of mystery.

GENERAL
▲ Fear, illusion, subconscious, hidden truths.
▼ Facing fears, uncovering hidden truths, intuition.

LOVE
▲ Facing fears and insecurities in love, hidden emotions, intuition.
▼ Deception in love, emotional manipulation, difficulty trusting yourself.

MONEY
▲ Hidden truths, emotional spending, facing financial fears.
▼ Uncovering deception, trusting your intuition, managing emotional spending.

CAREER
▲ Intuition, hidden truths, anxieties, facing fears, hiddenpotential.
▼ Confusion, insecurities, deception, manipulation by others, unclear career path.

HEALTH-WELLBEING
▲ Facing fears and anxieties, uncovering hidden health concerns, intuition.
▼ Deception, ignoring warning signs, difficulty trusting yourself.

SPIRITUALITY
▲ Intuition, spiritual mystery, subconscious.
▼ Deception, confusion, unresolved fears.

19 | NINETEEN
Joy, success, vitality

THE SUN .

The Sun

"JOY AND VITALITY"

Depicting a radiant sun, it symbolizes joy, vitality, and enlightenment.

Michael
Archangel

Fire
Element

Plexus
Chakras

Emotional
Domain

Sun
Planet

Joy, vitality, enlightenment	Creativity, vitality, optimism.	Purity, innocence, and clarity.	Life force, passion, energy.
YELLOW	**ORANGE**	**WHITE**	**RED**

SUN:
Radiant energy, enlightenment.

SUN-FACE:
Positive life force.

CHILD:
Innocence, carefree joy.

SUNFLOWERS:
Growth, warmth, creativity.

BANNER:
Victory, celebration of life.

RED FEATHER:
Vitality, passion.

HORSE:
Purity, untamed energy.

GENERAL
▲ Happiness, success, joy, vitality.

▼ Overconfidence, superficiality, arrogance.

LOVE
▲ Happiness and joy in love, success and fulfillment, celebration.

▼ Superficial relationships, arrogance, difficulty connecting deeply.

MONEY
▲ Success, achievement, financial security, reaping rewards.

▼ Overconfidence, superficiality, ignoring potential risks.

CAREER
▲ Success, achievement, recognition, clarity, joy in your work.

▼ Overconfidence, egotism, neglecting team collaboration, overlooking potential problems.

HEALTH-WELLBEING
▲ Joy, healing, feeling revitalized, experiencing good health.

▼ Overconfidence, ignoring potential health risks, superficiality.

SPIRITUALITY
▲ Spiritual joy, enlightenment, clarity.

▼ Ego, overexposure, hidden aspects.

20 | TWENTY
Renewal, awakening, reflection.

JUDGEMENT.

ANGEL:
Divine guidance, awakening.

RED ANGEL WINGS:
Passionate vitality.

TRUMPET:
Call to resurrection.

FLAG:
Victory, spiritual triumph.

PEOPLE:
Resurrection, collective awakening.

COFFINS:
Shedding old patterns.

SEA:
Collective unconscious, spiritual depth.

Judgement

"REBIRTH AND INNER CALLING"
Depicting angels blowing trumpets, it symbolizes awakening and answering the call from within.

Raphael
Archangel

Fire
Element

Throat
Chakras

Spiritual
Domain

Pluto
Planet

Spiritual awakening, truth, divine call.	Spiritual, purity, renewal.	Passion, energy, life force.	Divine energy, wisdom, success.
BLUE	**WHITE**	**RED**	**GOLD**

GENERAL
▲ Awakening, transformation, accountability, rebirth.

▼ Stagnation, fear of change, resistance to growth.

LOVE
▲ Awakening to your true needs in love, self-love, personal growth .

▼ Fear of growth, self-denial, avoiding responsibility.

MONEY
▲ Awakening, personal growth, taking responsibility for finances.

▼ Fear of growth, avoiding responsibility, living in denial.

CAREER
▲ Inner voice, reflection, taking accountability for career choices, transformation.

▼ Self-judgment, fear of change, resistance to self-improvement, neglecting career development.

HEALTH-WELLBEING
▲ Awakening, personal growth, taking responsibility for your health.

▼ Fear of growth, avoiding responsibility, living in denial.

SPIRITUALITY
▲ Spiritual awakening, reckoning, renewal.

▼ Self-judgment, avoidance, resistance to change.

21 | TWENTY-ONE
Completion, achievement, wholeness.

THE VVORLD.

DANCER:
Celebration, harmony.

PURPLE SASH:
Wisdom, mastery.

WANDS:
Balance, holistic understanding.

LAUREL WREATH:
Victory, achievement.

MAN, LION, EAGLE, BULL:
Cosmic harmony, universal alignment.

The World

"COMPLETION AND WHOLENESS"
Depicting a dancer within a wreath, it symbolizes the achievement of a cycle, completion, and spiritual enlightenment.

Uriel
Archangel

Earth
Element

Sacral
Chakras

Spiritual
Domain

Saturn
Planet

Transformation, spiritual completion. **PURPLE**	Growth, balance, harmony. **GREEN**
Enlightenment, fulfillment, wholeness **YELLOW**	Unity, spiritual understanding, completion **BLUE**

GENERAL
▲ Completion, achievement, fulfillment, integration.

▼ Missed opportunities, lack of closure, feeling unfulfilled.

LOVE
▲ Completion and satisfaction in love, achieving desires, feeling whole.

▼ Missed opportunities in love, lack of closure, dissatisfaction.

MONEY
▲ Completion, fulfillment, achieving financial goals, stability.

▼ Missed opportunities, lack of closure, dissatisfaction.

CAREER
▲ Completion, fulfillment, achieving career goals, celebration, legacy.

▼ Lack of closure, unfulfilled potential, missed opportunities, feeling stuck.

HEALTH-WELLBEING
▲ Completion, achieving overall well-being, feeling whole.

▼ Missed opportunities, neglecting long-term health goals, dissatisfaction.

SPIRITUALITY
▲ Spiritual completion, fulfillment, wholeness.

▼ Incompletion, unfinished business, lack of closure.

Cups
SUIT

Ace of Cups		Page of Cups	
Two of Cups		Knight of Cups	
Three of Cups		Queen of Cups	
Four of Cups		King of Cups	
Five of Cups			
Six of Cups			
Seven of Cups			
Eight of Cups			
Nine of Cups			
Ten of Cups			

1 | ACE
Beginnings, potential, new opportunities.

CHALICE:
Emotional fulfillment.

FIVE STREAMS OF WATER:
Overflowing emotions.

YODS:
Divine inspiration.

DOVE:
Peace, divine communication.

HAND AND CLOUD:
Spiritual blessing.

Ace of Cups

"OVERFLOWING EMOTIONS AND NEW BEGINNINGS"
Depicting a hand emerging from a cloud holding a cup overflowing with water, the card represents the pure essence of love and emotional fulfillment.

Gabriel
Archangel

Water
Element

Heart
Chakras

Emotional
Domain

Hearts
Traditional Cards

Purity, new beginnings, clarity.	Emotion, intuition, spirituality.	Growth, renewal, abundance.	Abundance, divine energy, enlightenment.
WHITE	**BLUE**	**GREEN**	**GOLD**

GENERAL

▲ New beginnings, joy, hope, emotional abundance.

▼ Stagnation, disappointment, emotional blockage.

LOVE

▲ New beginnings in love, emotional fulfillment, deep feelings.

▼ Emotional blockages, unrequited love, feeling drained.

MONEY

▲ New beginnings, emotional abundance, positive outlook on finances.

▼ Stagnation, disappointment, emotional blockages impacting financial decisions.

CAREER

▲ New career beginnings, emotional fulfillment in work, abundance of opportunities.

▼ Stagnation, lack of inspiration, neglecting emotional needs in work.

HEALTH-WELLBEING

▲ New beginnings, emotional abundance, positive outlook impacting health.

▼ Stagnation, emotional blockage, fear of abundance, neglecting emotional well-being.

SPIRITUALITY

▲ Divine love, emotional renewal, spiritual awakening.

▼ Blocked emotions, disconnection, lack of love.

2 | TWO
Balance, duality, partnerships, choices.

CHALICE:
Emotional connection.

CADUCEUS OF HERMES:
Balance, union.

SNAKES:
Harmonious duality.

WINGS:
Spiritual elevation.

Two of Cups

"MUTUAL CONNECTION AND HARMONY"
Featuring a depiction of two figures exchanging cups, it symbolizes mutual connection and emotional balance.

Gabriel
Archangel

Water
Element

Heart
Chakras

Emotional
Domain

Hearts
Traditional Cards

 Harmonious communication, peace, honesty.
BLUE

 Passionate connection, love, desire.
RED

 Emotional growth, harmony, balance.
GREEN

 Happiness , optimism, intellectual connection, shared goals.
YELLOW

GENERAL

▲ Partnership, connection, harmony, shared emotions.

▼ Miscommunication, disconnection, imbalance.

LOVE

▲ Partnership, mutual attraction, harmony in relationships.

▼ Miscommunication, imbalance, breakups or conflicts.

MONEY

▲ Partnership, shared resources, balanced financial agreements.

▼ Miscommunication, disconnection, imbalance in financial contributions.

CAREER

▲ Partnerships, collaboration, harmonious relationships with colleagues, balanced workload.

▼ Miscommunication, disconnection, conflict with colleagues, feeling undervalued.

HEALTH-WELLBEING

▲ Partnership, connection, balanced emotional relationships impacting health.

▼ Miscommunication, disconnection, imbalance in relationships impacting health.

SPIRITUALITY

▲ Soul connection, harmony, spiritual unity.

▼ Imbalance, broken bonds, spiritual disconnect.

3 | THREE
Growth, creativity, collaboration.

Three of Cups

"CELEBRATION AND JOYFUL CONNECTIONS"
Depicting three figures raising their cups in a joyful toast,
it symbolizes shared moments of happiness.

Gabriel
Archangel

Water
Element

Sacral
Chakras

Emotional
Domain

Hearts
Traditional Cards

Growth, abundance, emotional balance.	Enthusiasm, passion, excitement.	Harmony, communication, emotional depth.	Celebration, joy, friendship.
GREEN	**RED**	**BLUE**	**YELLOW**

DANCING MAIDENS:
Joyful celebration.

FLOWERS:
Blossoming friendships.

GRAPES:
Abundance, shared prosperity.

APPLES:
Harmony and unity.

BLUE SKY:
Uplifting atmosphere.

GENERAL

▲ Celebration, community, shared joy, laughter.

▼ Loneliness, exclusion, feeling out of place.

LOVE

▲ Celebration, joy, friendships turning into love.

▼ Overindulgence, love triangles, feeling left out.

MONEY

▲ Celebration, community, shared joy, receiving financial rewards.

▼ Loneliness, feeling excluded from financial opportunities.

CAREER

▲ Celebration, shared success, teamwork, enjoying work environment.

▼ Feeling excluded, isolation, lack of team spirit, neglecting networking.

HEALTH-WELLBEING

▲ Celebration, community, shared joy, positive emotions benefiting health.

▼ Loneliness, feeling excluded, neglecting social connections impacting health.

SPIRITUALITY

▲ Spiritual celebration, friendship, connection.

▼ Disharmony, disruption, isolation.

4 | FOUR
Stability, structure, foundation.

Current Situation

Four of Cups

"CONTEMPLATION AND EMOTIONAL WITHDRAWAL"

Depicting a figure sitting under a tree, seemingly uninterested in the offered cups, it symbolizes emotional withdrawal and introspective moments.

Gabriel
Archangel

Water
Element

Plexus
Chakras

Emotional
Domain

Hearts
Traditional Cards

Emotional growth, healing, renewal.
GREEN

Reflection, contemplation, inner peace.
BLUE

Detachment, introspection, neutrality.
GREY

Clarity, positivity, new perspectives.
YELLOW

HAND OF GOD:
Spiritual offering.

TREE:
Stability, grounding.

MOUNTAINS:
Overcoming challenges.

BLUE SKY:
Clarity and insight.

GENERAL

▲ Emotional apathy, dissatisfaction, boredom, stagnation.

▼ Renewed interest, opening up to possibilities, overcoming emotional blocks.

LOVE

▲ Contemplation, reevaluating relationships, feeling unfulfilled.

▼ New opportunities in love, awakening to possibilities, moving on.

MONEY

▲ Emotional apathy, dissatisfaction, boredom, neglecting financial planning.

▼ Renewed interest, opening up to possibilities, overcoming emotional blocks.

CAREER

▲ Dissatisfaction, boredom, uninspired by work, seeking new opportunities.

▼ Renewed interest, overcoming apathy, finding meaning in work.

HEALTH-WELLBEING

▲ Emotional apathy, dissatisfaction, boredom, neglecting emotional needs impacting health.

▼ Renewed interest, opening up to possibilities, overcoming emotional blocks.

SPIRITUALITY

▲ Spiritual contemplation, reflection, withdrawal.

▼ Apathy, discontentment, ignoring spirituality.

5 | FIVE
Change, conflict, instability, challenge

Five of Cups

"LOSS AND GRIEVING"

Featuring a figure mourning over spilled cups while three remain standing, it symbolizes grieving and emotional turbulence.

Gabriel
Archangel

Water
Element

Heart
Chakras

Emotional
Domain

Hearts
Traditional Cards

 Loss, detachment, introspection.
GREY

 Passion, intensity, emotional healing.
RED

 Grief, mourning, transformation.
BLACK

 Sorrow, reflection, emotional depth.
BLUE

SPILLED WINE:
Loss, disappointment.

RIVER:
Flow of emotions, healing.

BRIDGE:
Broken connection, rebuilding.

CASTLE:
Stability, potential refuge.

CLOAK:
Mourning, emotional protection.

GRAY SKY:
Somber mood, potential for clarity

GENERAL

▲ Loss, grief, disappointment, emotional pain.

▼ Healing, acceptance, moving forward.

LOVE

▲ Regret, sorrow, focusing on past relationships.

▼ Healing, forgiveness, moving forward from past hurts.

MONEY

▲ Loss, grief, disappointment, emotional impact on finances.

▼ Healing, acceptance, moving forward, making wise financial decisions.

CAREER

▲ Loss, disappointment, setbacks, emotional impact on career.

▼ Resilience, learning from mistakes, moving forward with optimism.

HEALTH-WELLBEING

▲ Loss, grief, emotional pain, impacting physical health.

▼ Healing, acceptance, moving forward, finding emotional support.

SPIRITUALITY

▲ Loss, grief, emotional transformation.

▼ Healing, recovery, moving forward

6 | SIX
Harmony, balance, resolution.

Six of Cups

"NOSTALGIA AND INNOCENT JOY"
Depicting two figures exchanging cups, it symbolizes the purity of childhood memories and simple pleasures.

Gabriel *Archangel* | **Water** *Element* | **Heart** *Chakras* | **Emotional** *Domain* | **Hearts** *Traditional Cards*

YELLOW	BLUE	WHITE	GREEN
Nostalgia, childhood memories.	Introspection, nostalgia, peace.	Purity, innocence, clarity, reflexion.	Emotional growth, innocence, nostalgia.

CHILDREN:
Innocence, playfulness.

WHITE FLOWER:
Purity, friendship.

VILLAGE:
Community, shared experiences.

INSCRIPTION X ON PILLAR:
Symbolic completion, return to innocence.

GENERAL
▲ Nostalgia, childhood memories, innocence, past happiness.

▼ Dwelling on the past, emotional immaturity, inability to move on.

LOVE
▲ Nostalgia, past relationships, childhood sweethearts.

▼ Living in the past, difficulty moving on, unrealistic expectations.

MONEY
▲ Nostalgia, childhood memories, past financial security.

▼ Dwelling on past successes, neglecting current financial reality.

CAREER
▲ Nostalgia, past positive work experiences, seeking similar environment.

▼ Dwelling on the past, neglecting present opportunities, emotional immaturity.

HEALTH-WELLBEING
▲ Nostalgia, past emotional connections impacting present health.

▼ Dwelling on the past, neglecting present emotional needs, emotional immaturity.

SPIRITUALITY
▲ Spiritual nostalgia, innocence, memories.

▼ Stagnation, clinging to the past, avoidance.

7 | SEVEN
Strategy, introspection, reflection, spirituality.

"ILLUSIONS AND CHOICES"
Featuring a figure surrounded by various images emerging from cups,
it symbolizes the myriad possibilities and illusions that can cloud judgment.

Gabriel *Archangel*	**Water** *Element*	**Third Eye** *Chakras*	**Emotional** *Domain*	**Hearts** *Traditional Cards*

BLUE	RED	WHITE	YELLOW
Imagination, dreams, possibilities.	Illusions, temptations, intensity.	Clarity, spiritual insights, choices.	Optimism, decision-making, mental clarity.

HUMAN FACE:
Choices, options.

LAUREL WREATH:
Victory, aspirations.

GHOST:
Illusions, discernment.

SNAKE:
Temptation, caution.

CASTLE:
Security, stability.

JEWELS:
Material wealth, abundance.

DRAGON:
Challenges, obstacles.

GENERAL

▲ Imagination, daydreaming, possibility, exploration.

▼ Confusion, indecision, unrealistic expectations.

LOVE

▲ Many choices, fantasy, romantic dreams.

▼ Clarity, making decisions, avoiding illusions in love.

MONEY

▲ Imagination, daydreaming, unrealistic financial expectations.

▼ Confusion, indecision, impulsive financial choices.

CAREER

▲ Daydreams, unrealistic expectations, exploring career options, uncertainty.

▼ Confusion, indecisiveness, neglecting practicalities, impulsive career choices.

HEALTH-WELLBEING

▲ Daydreams, unrealistic expectations, exploring emotional needs, impacting health.

▼ Confusion, indecisiveness, neglecting practical health choices.

SPIRITUALITY

▲ Spiritual choices, imagination, vision.

▼ Confusion, illusions, misguidance.

8 | EIGHT
Power, progress, movement.

Eight of Cups

"EMOTIONAL DEPARTURE AND SEEKING MORE"
Depicting a figure walking away from a stack of cups,
it symbolizes the journey to find emotional satisfaction beyond
current circumstances.

Gabriel
Archangel

Water
Element

Plexus
Chakras

Emotional
Domain

Hearts
Traditional Cards

 BLUE — Depth, emotion, and introspection.

 GREY — Detachment, letting go, moving on.

 BROWN — Earthiness, grounding, stability.

 RED — Passionate pursuit of meaning, determination.

RED CLOAK:
Passion and determination on the transformative journey.

ECLIPSED SUN AND MOON:
Signifying a period of transition and change.

NIGHT-TIME SETTING:
Representing the end of one phase and the beginning of another.

MOUNTAINS:
Indicating challenges to overcome on the journey.

RIVER:
Symbolizing the flow of emotions and the continuous quest for self-discovery.

GENERAL

▲ Letting go, moving on, emotional detachment, seeking new experiences.

▼ Escapism, avoidance, difficulty facing emotions.

LOVE

▲ Leaving a relationship, searching for deeper meaning.

▼ Fear of change, staying in unfulfilling relationships, returning.

MONEY

▲ Letting go, emotional detachment, moving on from financial hardship.

▼ Escapism, avoidance, difficulty facing financial challenges.

CAREER

▲ Letting go, moving on from unfulfilling career, following true calling.

▼ Escapism, avoidance, neglecting current responsibilities, delaying important decisions.

HEALTH-WELLBEING

▲ Letting go, moving on from emotional pain, impacting health.

▼ Escapism, avoidance, difficulty processing emotions, neglecting healthy coping mechanisms.

SPIRITUALITY

▲ Spiritual journey, seeking truth, emotional growth.

▼ Fear of change, holding on, resistance.

9 | NINE
Fulfillment, nearing completion, introspection.

Nine of Cups

"EMOTIONAL FULFILLMENT AND CONTENTMENT"
Featuring a figure surrounded by nine cups,
it symbolizes abundance and the attainment of emotional satisfaction.

Gabriel
Archangel

Water
Element

Plexus
Chakras

Emotional
Domain

Hearts
Traditional Cards

Prosperity, abundance, wish fulfillment	Emotional fulfillment, inner peace	Clarity, transparency, harmony unity	Passionate satisfaction, desire fulfillment
YELLOW	**BLUE**	**WHITE**	**RED**

MAN IN RED HAT:
Contentment.

CUPS ON DISPLAY:
Emotional fulfillment.

CURTAIN:
Revealing satisfaction.

BENCH:
Stability, comfort.

GENERAL
▲ Emotional fulfillment, contentment, satisfaction, wishes granted.

▼ Self-indulgence, superficiality, lack of deeper meaning.

LOVE
▲ Emotional satisfaction, wishes fulfilled, contentment in love.

▼ Overindulgence, complacency, superficial happiness.

MONEY
▲ Emotional fulfillment, contentment, gratitude for financial blessings.

▼ Self-indulgence, superficiality, neglecting ethical considerations.

CAREER
▲ Emotional fulfillment, contentment with career, achieving work-life balance.

▼ Self-indulgence, superficiality, neglecting ethical considerations, neglecting growth opportunities.

HEALTH-WELLBEING
▲ Emotional fulfillment, contentment, gratitude, positive impact on health.

▼ Self-indulgence, superficiality, neglecting deeper emotional needs, neglecting physical health.

SPIRITUALITY
▲ Spiritual contentment, emotional fulfillment, satisfaction.

▼ Complacency, smugness, unfulfilled desires.

Current Situation

10 | TEN
Completion, culmination, new cycles.

Ten of Cups

"HARMONY AND EMOTIONAL BLISS"
Depicting a happy family surrounded by cups, it symbolizes the attainment of emotional fulfillment and domestic harmony.

Gabriel
Archangel

Water
Element

Heart
Chakras

Emotional
Domain

Hearts
Traditional Cards

GREEN	BLUE	YELLOW	PINK
Family bonds, emotional growth, abundance.	Emotional fulfillment, contentment.	Joy, happiness, fulfillment.	Love, compassion, emotional connection.

FAMILY:
Unity, connection.

RAINBOW:
Joy, blessings.

COTTAGE:
Comfort, security.

TREES:
Stability, growth.

RIVER:
Emotional flow, continuity.

GENERAL
▲ Family, love, emotional fulfillment, deep connection.

▼ Emotional isolation, family issues, unfulfilled desires.

LOVE
▲ Lasting happiness, family harmony, fulfillment in love.

▼ Disconnection, family disputes, lack of emotional support.

MONEY
▲ Family, love, emotional fulfillment leading to financial stability.

▼ Emotional isolation, neglecting family's financial needs, unfulfilled desires.

CAREER
▲ Shared goals, family-oriented work environment, feeling valued and supported.

▼ Feeling disconnected, neglecting family needs due to work, unfulfilled emotional needs.

HEALTH-WELLBEING
▲ Family, love, deep emotional connection, impacting health and well-being.

▼ Feeling disconnected, family issues impacting health, unfulfilled emotional needs.

SPIRITUALITY
▲ Spiritual harmony, family, divine connection.

▼ Disharmony, broken dreams, instability.

COURT CARD | PAGE
Represent beginnings, learning, and messages.

PAGE of CUPS.

Page of Cups

"CREATIVITY AND EMOTIONAL MESSAGES"
Depicting a figure holding a cup with a fish emerging, it symbolizes the potential for creative inspiration and emotional exploration.

Gabriel	Water	Heart	Emotional	Hearts
Archangel	*Element*	*Chakras*	*Domain*	*Traditional Cards*

BLUE	WHITE	GOLD	GREY
Intuitive messages, emotional depth, communication.	Purity, innocence, receptivity.	Creative inspiration, divine guidance, intuition.	Calm, detachment, objectivity, maturity.

CUP:
Emotional receptivity.

BLUE FISH:
Intuition, creativity.

OCEAN:
Deep emotions, subconscious.

LOTUS FLOWERS:
Purity, spiritual growth.

BLUE FEATHER:
Creative inspiration, communication.

GENERAL
▲ Sensitivity, intuition, new emotional experiences, creativity.

▼ Emotional immaturity, impulsiveness, naivety.

LOVE
▲ New romantic messages, creative love expressions, infatuation.

▼ Emotional immaturity, insecurity, rejection of love.

MONEY
▲ Sensitivity, intuition, new emotional experiences, exploring creative financial options.

▼ Emotional immaturity, impulsiveness, naivety in financial matters.

CAREER
▲ Sensitivity, intuition, exploring creative solutions, emotional intelligence.

▼ Emotional immaturity, impulsiveness, naivety in work relationships, unrealistic expectations.

HEALTH-WELLBEING
▲ Sensitivity, intuition, exploring emotional needs, impacting health.

▼ Emotional immaturity, impulsiveness, naivety, neglecting healthy emotional expression.

SPIRITUALITY
▲ Spiritual exploration, curiosity, creativity.

▼ Emotional immaturity, rejection, confusion.

COURT CARD | KNIGHT
Symbolize action, adventure, and movement.

Knight of Cups

"ROMANTIC PURSUITS AND EMOTIONAL QUESTS"
Depicting a knight on horseback holding a cup, it symbolizes the arrival of emotional opportunities and romantic adventures.

| **Gabriel** *Archangel* | **Water** *Element* | **Heart** *Chakras* | **Emotional** *Domain* | **Hearts** *Traditional Cards* |

BLUE	SILVER	GOLD	RED
Emotional maturity, intuition, depth of feeling.	Reflective, intuitive insights, emotional balance.	Spiritual growth, enlightenment, divine connection.	Passionate pursuit, romantic energy, emotional intensity.

ARMOR:
Emotional protection.

HORSE:
Movement, pursuit.

WINGS:
Romantic idealism.

FISH:
Intuition, depth.

RIVER:
Emotional flow.

MOUNTAIN:
Challenges, perseverance.

TREES:
Stability, growth.

GENERAL

▲ Idealism, romance, charm, artistic expression.

▼ Manipulation, emotional infidelity, unrealistic expectations.

LOVE
▲ Romantic proposals, charm, idealistic love.

▼ Unrealistic expectations, moodiness, unfulfilled promises.

MONEY

▲ Idealism, romance, charm, unrealistic financial expectations.

▼ Manipulation, emotional infidelity, deceptive financial practices.

CAREER
▲ Idealism, charm, inspiring others, pursuing creative career visions.

▼ Manipulation, emotional infidelity, using charm for personal gain, unrealistic expectations.

HEALTH-WELLBEING

▲ Idealism, romance, charm, unrealistic expectations impacting health.

▼ Manipulation, emotional infidelity, deceptive relationships impacting health.

SPIRITUALITY

▲ Spiritual inspiration, romance, emotional adventure.

▼ Moodiness, emotional confusion, unstable emotions.

COURT CARD | QUEEN
Represent nurturing, authority, and intuition.

QUEEN of CUPS.

Queen of Cups

"EMOTIONAL INTUITION AND COMPASSION"

Depicting a queen with a cup in hand, it symbolizes emotional wisdom, intuition, and compassion.

Gabriel	**Water**	**Heart**	**Emotional**	**Hearts**
Archangel	*Element*	*Chakras*	*Domain*	*Traditional Cards*

Emotional intelligence, depth of compassion.	Reflective wisdom, intuitive receptivity.	Purity, spiritual insight, emotional clarity.	Emotional sensitivity, compassion, harmony, peace
BLUE	**SILVER**	**WHITE**	**PINK**

ORNATE CHALICE:
Emotional receptivity.

CROWN:
Emotional sovereignty.

THRONE:
Emotional stability.

ANGELS, CHERUBS:
Divine guidance.

CLIFFS:
Navigating challenges.

STONES:
Grounded foundation.

SEA:
Profound emotional insight.

GENERAL

▲ Compassion, intuition, nurturing, emotional intelligence.

▼ Overemotional, manipulative, martyr complex.

LOVE

▲ Compassionate love, emotional stability, nurturing.

▼ Emotional insecurity, dependency, being overly sensitive.

MONEY

▲ Compassion, intuition, nurturing, managing finances with empathy.

▼ Overemotional, manipulative, neglecting financial responsibility.

CAREER

▲ Compassion, empathy, nurturing work environment, providing emotional support.

▼ Overemotional, codependency, manipulative behavior, neglecting healthy boundaries.

HEALTH-WELLBEING

▲ Compassion, empathy, intuition, emotional intelligence, balancing emotions for health.

▼ Overemotional, codependency, manipulative behavior, neglecting healthy boundaries impacting health.

SPIRITUALITY

▲ Intuition, compassion, spiritual guidance.

▼ Overemotional, lack of control, vulnerability.

COURT CARD | KING
Symbolize mastery, authority, and control.

KING of CUPS.

King of Cups

"EMOTIONAL MASTERY AND COMPASSIONATE LEADERSHIP"
Depicting a king seated on a throne with a cup, it symbolizes emotional balance, wisdom, and compassionate leadership.

Gabriel *Archangel*
Water *Element*
Heart *Chakras*
Emotional *Domain*
Hearts *Traditional Cards*

BLUE — Emotional mastery, intuition, depth of understanding.

GREY — Emotional balance, neutrality, introspection.

GOLD — Inner abundance, emotional fulfillment.

YELLOW — Wisdom, clarity, optimism, positivity.

THRONE IN THE SEA:
Emotional stability.

SCEPTER:
Authority in emotions.

CHALICE:
Spiritual connection.

DOLPHIN:
Intelligent balance.

FISH:
Emotional depth.

RED SHIP:
Navigating challenges.

STORMY SEA:
Mastery in turbulent emotions.

GENERAL
▲ Emotional maturity, stability, wisdom, guidance.

▼ Repressed emotions, coldness, controlling behavior.

LOVE
▲ Mature love, emotional balance, supportive partner.

▼ Emotional manipulation, volatility, lack of control in love.

MONEY
▲ Emotional maturity, stability, wisdom, providing emotional support and guidance.

▼ Repressed emotions, coldness, controlling financial decisions.

CAREER
▲ Emotional maturity, stability, wisdom, guiding and supporting others.

▼ Repressed emotions, coldness, controlling behavior, neglecting emotional needs of others.

HEALTH-WELLBEING
▲ Emotional maturity, stability, wisdom, providing emotional support for health.

▼ Repressed emotions, coldness, controlling behavior, neglecting self-care and emotional needs.

SPIRITUALITY
▲ Emotional stability, spiritual wisdom, compassionate leadership.

▼ Suppression, manipulation, lack of empathy.

Pentacles
SUIT

1 | ACE
Beginnings, potential, new opportunities.

Ace of Pentacles

"MANIFESTATION AND NEW BEGINNINGS"
Depicting a hand emerging from a cloud, holding a pentacle surrounded by lush vegetation, it symbolizes the potential for material abundance and the manifestation of tangible goals.

| **Uriel** *Archangel* | **Earth** *Element* | **Root** *Chakras* | **Physical** *Domain* | **Clubs** *Traditional Cards* |

GREEN — Growth, prosperity, abundance.

GOLD — Material wealth, divine connection.

BROWN — Grounding, stability, practicality.

WHITE — Purity, new beginnings, spiritual alignment.

CLOUDS:
Divine blessings.

HAND OF GOD:
Higher influence.

GARDEN:
Fertility, abundance.

ROSE:
legant manifestation.

LILY OF THE VALLEY:
Purity, prosperity.

ARCHWAY:
Opportunity, success.

PATH:
Clear journey.

GENERAL
▲ New beginnings, security, stability, manifestation.
▼ Stagnation, lack of opportunity, feeling stuck.

LOVE
▲ New beginnings in a stable relationship, prosperity in love, long-term potential.
▼ Missed opportunities, instability in relationships, financial strain affecting love.

MONEY
▲ New beginnings, financial opportunities, manifestation of abundance, stable foundation.
▼ Stagnation, lack of opportunity, feeling stuck, self-doubt about finances.

CAREER
▲ Manifestation of success, stable foundation, new career beginnings, security.
▼ Stagnation, lack of opportunity, feeling stuck, self-doubt about abilities.

HEALTH-WELLBEING
▲ Manifestation of physical wellness, new beginnings, healthy foundation.
▼ Stagnation, lack of opportunity, neglecting self-care, feeling stuck.

SPIRITUALITY
▲ Spiritual opportunity, new beginnings, manifestation.
▼ Missed opportunities, spiritual blockage, stagnation.

2 | TWO
Balance, duality, partnerships, choices.

Two of Pentacles

"BALANCE AND ADAPTABILITY"
Featuring a figure juggling two pentacles with a sea in the background, it symbolizes the need to balance material responsibilities and remain adaptable in the face of change.

Uriel
Archangel

Earth
Element

Root
Chakras

Physical
Domain

Clubs
Traditional Cards

GREEN	YELLOW	BLUE	RED
Harmony, balance, growth.	Flexibility, joy, optimism.	Stability, calmness, measured decision-making.	ynamic balance, adaptability, energy.

INFINITY SYMBOL:
Cyclical challenges.

JUGGLER:
Balancing responsibilities.

RAISED LEFT FOOT:
Active adaptability.

SEA:
Dynamic life challenges.

SHIPS:
External influences.

TALL HAT:
Confidence in management.

GENERAL
▲ Juggling resources, financial planning, adaptation.
▼ Uncertainty, instability, feeling overwhelmed.

LOVE
▲ Balance in relationships, managing love and other responsibilities, adaptability.
▼ Overwhelm, juggling too much, neglecting relationship needs.

MONEY
▲ Juggling resources, budgeting, adaptability, managing multiple financial demands.
▼ Uncertainty, instability, feeling overwhelmed, neglecting priorities.

CAREER
▲ Balancing priorities, juggling workload, managing resources effectively, resourcefulness.
▼ Uncertainty, instability, feeling overwhelmed, neglecting important tasks.

HEALTH-WELLBEING
▲ Balancing work and health, managing time and resources, juggling priorities.
▼ Uncertainty, instability, feeling overwhelmed, neglecting self-care.

SPIRITUALITY
▲ Balance, flexibility, spiritual adaptability.
▼ Imbalance, overwhelm, disruption.

3 | THREE
Growth, creativity, collaboration.

Three of Pentacles

"COLLABORATION AND MASTERY"

Depicting a figure working on a project with two others, it symbolizes the mastery achieved through collaborative efforts in the material realm.

Uriel *Archangel* | **Earth** *Element* | **Root** *Chakras* | **Physical** *Domain* | **Clubs** *Traditional Cards*

BROWN — Practical skills, craftsmanship, stability.
YELLOW — Creativity, optimism, success.
BLUE — Shared goals, excellence, expertise.
GREY — Collaboration, neutrality, teamwork.

SCULPTOR:
Skilled craftsmanship.

DARK INTERIOR:
Focused workspace.

APRON:
Commitment to work.

BENCH:
Stable foundation.

TOOLS:
Precision and expertise.

ENGRAVINGS:
Attention to details.

GENERAL
▲ Teamwork, collaboration, skilled craftsmanship, mastery.
▼ Lack of direction, feeling undervalued, procrastination.

LOVE
▲ Teamwork, building a future together, collaboration in relationships.
▼ Lack of cooperation, misalignment of goals, feeling undervalued.

MONEY
▲ Collaboration, skilled work, shared ventures, reaping financial rewards.
▼ Lack of direction, feeling undervalued, procrastination, neglecting individual contributions.

CAREER
▲ Teamwork, collaboration, skilled work, shared knowledge, learning from others.
▼ Lack of direction, feeling undervalued, neglecting individual contributions, working in silos.

HEALTH-WELLBEING
▲ Collaborative healing, sharing knowledge and expertise, learning from others.
▼ Lack of direction, feeling undervalued, neglecting individual needs.

SPIRITUALITY
▲ Spiritual collaboration, teamwork, learning.
▼ Lack of cooperation, misalignment, disconnection.

4 | FOUR
Stability, structure, foundation.

Four of Pentacles

"STABILITY AND HOLDING ON"
Depicting a figure holding onto pentacles with a stable posture, it symbolizes the desire for stability and security in the material realm.

Uriel
Archangel

Earth
Element

Root
Chakras

Physical
Domain

Clubs
Traditional Cards

Possessiveness, desire for control, power	Material wealth, stability, prosperity.	Stability, calmness, conservative approach.	Security, practicality, grounding.
RED	**GOLD**	**BLUE**	**BROWN**

PENTACLES:
Material wealth.

CITY/VILLAGE:
External world.

CROWN:
Authority and control.

TETRAGRAMMATON:
Balance with spirituality.

UNTIED SHOES:
Potential vulnerability.

GENERAL

▲ Security, possessiveness, materialism, stability.

▼ Greed, hoarding, fear of loss.

LOVE

▲ Security, holding onto a relationship tightly, possessiveness.

▼ Letting go, insecurity, fear of loss.

MONEY

▲ Security, possessiveness, careful spending, material stability.

▼ Greed, hoarding, fear of loss, neglecting investments.

CAREER

▲ Financial security, careful planning, responsible decisions, possessiveness.

▼ Greed, hoarding, fear of loss, neglecting investments, overwork.

HEALTH-WELLBEING

▲ Security and comfort through mindful spending, prioritizing health.

▼ Greed, hoarding, neglecting emotional well-being, overindulgence.

SPIRITUALITY

▲ Stability, spiritual security, conservatism.

▼ Greed, attachment, spiritual rigidity.

5 | FIVE
Change, conflict, instability, challenge

Five of Pentacles

"HARDSHIP AND FINANCIAL STRUGGLE"
Featuring figures in the cold outside a church, it symbolizes the challenges of facing financial difficulties and seeking assistance.

| **Uriel** *Archangel* | **Earth** *Element* | **Root** *Chakras* | **Physical** *Domain* | **Clubs** *Traditional Cards* |

BLUE — Stability, hope, conservative approach.

RED — Struggle, emotional intensity, financial distress.

YELLOW — Optimism, resilience, mental agility.

BLACK — Isolation, confront and overcome fears, courage.

CHURCH WINDOW:
Symbol of refuge.

CRIPPLE:
Vulnerability, limitation.

CRUTCHES:
External support.

SNOW:
Harsh conditions.

GENERAL
▲ Loss, material hardship, feeling alone, vulnerability.

▼ Unexpected help, resilience, resourcefulness.

LOVE
▲ Struggles in relationships, feeling left out, emotional or financial hardship.

▼ Recovery, improved circumstances, support in love.

MONEY
▲ Loss, hardship, unexpected expenses, feeling unprepared.

▼ Unexpected support, resilience, resourcefulness, finding new financial opportunities.

CAREER
▲ Unexpected challenges, financial difficulties, feeling unprepared, resilience.

▼ Unexpected support, resourcefulness, finding new opportunities, learning from setbacks.

HEALTH-WELLBEING
▲ Unexpected challenges, adapting to setbacks, finding resilience.

▼ Unexpected support, resourcefulness, finding new health resources.

SPIRITUALITY
▲ Spiritual struggle, hard times, isolation.

▼ Recovery, reconnection, spiritual renewal.

6 | SIX
Harmony, balance, resolution

Six of Pentacles

"GENEROSITY AND FAIR EXCHANGE"
Depicting a figure sharing coins with others, it symbolizes the principles of giving and receiving in a balanced manner.

Uriel
Archangel

Earth
Element

Root
Chakras

Physical
Domain

Clubs
Traditional Cards

GREEN — Generosity, prosperity, sharing.

GOLD — Material success, abundance, generosity.

RED — Compassion, giving, charity.

GREY — Balance, fairness, impartiality.

SCALES:
Balanced distribution.

RED CLOAK:
Compassion and empathy.

4 COINS:
Shared material resources.

CASTLE:
Symbol of prosperity.

BENEDICTION:
Positive affirmation.

BANDAGE:
Tangible assistance.

RED TICKET:
Request for help.

GENERAL
▲ Generosity, charity, sharing, receiving support.

▼ Exploitation, imbalance, taking advantage.

LOVE
▲ Generosity, balanced give-and-take, supportive relationships.

▼ Imbalance, strings attached, one-sided giving.

MONEY
▲ Generosity, sharing resources, receiving financial support, contributing to community.

▼ Exploitation, imbalance, taking advantage, neglecting financial boundaries.

CAREER
▲ Generosity, supporting others' career growth, receiving support, contribution to team success.

▼ Exploitation, imbalance, taking advantage, neglecting financial boundaries.

HEALTH-WELLBEING
▲ Generosity, supporting others' health, receiving support.

▼ Exploitation, imbalance, taking advantage, neglecting healthy boundaries.

SPIRITUALITY
▲ Generosity, spiritual charity, sharing.

▼ Greed, imbalance, selfishness.

7 | SEVEN
Strategy, introspection, reflection, spirituality.

Seven of Pentacles

"PATIENCE AND GROWTH"
Featuring a figure observing the growth of pentacles on a plant, it symbolizes the need for patience in waiting for the fruition of one's efforts.

Uriel
Archangel

Earth
Element

Root
Chakras

Physical
Domain

Clubs
Traditional Cards

Growth, patience, cultivation.
GREEN

Hard work, investment, practical efforts.
BROWN

Stability, patience, conservative approach.
BLUE

Evaluation, assessment, planning.
YELLOW

HOE:
Cultivation and effort.

GRAY SKY:
Period of waiting.

GRAPEVINE:
Potential abundance.

GENERAL
▲ Hard work, patience, delayed rewards, perseverance.

▼ Impatience, lack of focus, giving up too soon.

LOVE
▲ Patience, long-term investment in love, evaluating progress.

▼ Impatience, lack of reward, feeling stagnant.

MONEY
▲ Hard work, patience, delayed financial rewards, perseverance.

▼ Impatience, lack of focus, giving up easily, neglecting long-term financial goals.

CAREER
▲ Hard work, patience, delayed rewards, long-term vision, perseverance.

▼ Impatience, lack of focus, giving up easily, neglecting ongoing effort.

HEALTH-WELLBEING
▲ Patience, perseverance, delayed rewards, long-term health goals.

▼ Impatience, lack of focus, giving up easily, neglecting preventative care.

SPIRITUALITY
▲ Patience, spiritual growth, long-term view.

▼ Impatience, stagnation, disappointment.

8 | EIGHT
Power, progress, movement.

Eight of Pentacles

"DILIGENCE AND MASTERY"

Featuring a figure diligently working on pentacles, it symbolizes the dedication and effort required to master one's craft in the material realm.

Uriel
Archangel

Earth
Element

Root
Chakras

Physical
Domain

Clubs
Traditional Cards

Skill development, craftsmanship, hard work.
BROWN

Mastery, success, achievement.
GOLD

Passion for work, diligence, commitment
RED

Focus, dedication, precision.
GREY

HAMMER:
Precision and force.

CHISEL:
Meticulous craftsmanship.

APRON:
Hands-on dedication.

BENCH:
Stable workspace.

CASTLE:
Achievement and growth.

GENERAL

 ▲ Apprenticeship, mastery, dedication, honing skills.

▼ Lack of motivation, boredom, feeling directionless.

LOVE

 ▲ Effort and dedication in love, working on the relationship, commitment.

▼ Lack of effort, neglect, repetitive problems.

MONEY

▲ Apprenticeship, dedication, honing financial skills, mastery.

▼ Lack of motivation, boredom, feeling stuck, neglecting financial self-improvement.

CAREER

 ▲ Apprenticeship, dedication, honing skills, mastering craft, commitment to learning.

▼ Lack of motivation, boredom, feeling stuck, neglecting skill development.

HEALTH-WELLBEING

▲ Self-improvement, dedication to learning and mastering healthy habits.

▼ Lack of motivation, boredom, feeling stuck, neglecting self-care.

SPIRITUALITY

 ▲ Dedication, spiritual development, hard work.

▼ Lack of focus, mediocrity, spiritual disinterest.

9 | NINE
Fulfillment, nearing completion, introspection.

Nine of Pentacles
"ABUNDANCE AND SELF-SUFFICIENCY"

Depicting a figure in a flourishing garden with a falcon, it symbolizes the rewards of hard work and the achievement of material abundance.

Uriel
Archangel

Earth
Element

Root
Chakras

Physical
Domain

Clubs
Traditional Cards

Prosperity, self-sufficiency, abundance	Wealth, accomplishment, luxury.	Independence, peace, refinement, elegance.	Passion for life, abundance, success.
GREEN	**GOLD**	**WHITE**	**RED**

ESTATE:
Prosperity and success.

SNAIL:
Steady progress.

FALCON:
Mastery and control.

YELLOW GLOVE:
Precision and discipline.

VENUS SYMBOLS:
Harmonious balance.

TWO TREES:
Stability and support.

GENERAL

▲ Self-sufficiency, security, comfort, independence.

▼ Self-indulgence, materialism, neglecting responsibilities.

LOVE

▲ Independence, enjoying solitude, self-sufficiency in love.

▼ Loneliness, dependency, superficial relationships.

MONEY

▲ Self-sufficiency, financial security, comfort, independence, reaping financial rewards.

▼ Self-indulgence, materialism, neglecting financial responsibilities, feeling unfulfilled.

CAREER

▲ Self-sufficiency, security, comfort, independence, reaping rewards of hard work.

▼ Self-indulgence, materialism, neglecting responsibilities, feeling unfulfilled.

HEALTH-WELLBEING

▲ Self-sufficiency, security, enjoying fruits of healthy choices, balance.

▼ Self-indulgence, materialism, neglecting preventive care, neglecting mental health.

SPIRITUALITY

▲ Spiritual independence, fulfillment, gratitude.

▼ Isolation, financial dependence, loneliness.

Current Situation

Ten of Pentacles

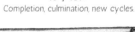

10 | TEN

Completion, culmination, new cycles.

"LEGACY AND FAMILY WEALTH"

Depicting a family under an arch with pentacles, it symbolizes the establishment of a secure and prosperous family legacy.

Uriel	Earth	Root	Physical	Clubs
Archangel	*Element*	*Chakras*	*Domain*	*Traditional Cards*

BROWN	GOLD	BLUE	GREEN
Family, prosperity, abundance.	Wealth, financial success, inheritance.	Legacy, tradition, financial stability, security.	Family, prosperity, abundance.

OLD MAN:
Wisdom and experience.

CHILD:
Future and growth.

COUPLE:
Unity and partnership.

TREE OF LIFE:
Family interconnectedness.

SCALES:
Balance and fairness.

TOWER:
Stability and achievement.

DOGS:
Loyalty and companionship.

GENERAL

▲ Legacy, generational wealth, long-term success, fulfillment.

▼ Lack of vision, instability, neglecting family.

LOVE

▲ Long-term commitment, family harmony, legacy of love.

▼ Family conflict, instability, challenges in building a future together.

MONEY

▲ Legacy, generational wealth, long-term financial success, stability.

▼ Lack of vision, instability, neglecting family's financial needs, unfulfilled financial desires.

CAREER

▲ Legacy, generational success, long-term stability, achieving career aspirations.

▼ Lack of vision, instability, neglecting family's needs, unfulfilled desires.

HEALTH-WELLBEING

▲ Legacy of healthy habits, long-term well-being, stability.

▼ Lack of vision, neglecting family's health needs, unfulfilled desires.

SPIRITUALITY

▲ Spiritual legacy, family traditions, continuity.

▼ Broken legacy, instability, disrupted traditions.

COURT CARD | PAGE
Represent beginnings, learning, and messages.

PAGE of PENTACLES.

Page of Pentacles

"PRACTICALITY AND NEW BEGINNINGS"
Depicting a figure with a pentacle in a lush landscape, it symbolizes the potential for practical endeavors and the initiation of tangible projects.

Uriel
Archangel

Earth
Element

Root
Chakras

Physical
Domain

Clubs
Traditional Cards

Growth, learning, practical skills.	Passion for learning, fiery curiosity, zeal.	Intellectual curiosity, analytical thinking.	Curiosity, intellectual exploration, new opportunities.
GREEN	**RED**	**BLUE**	**YELLOW**

RED HAT:
Bold enthusiasm.

PLOWED FIELDS:
Fertile ground.

YELLOW SKY:
Optimism and positivity.

TREES AND MOUNTAINS:
Natural challenges and opportunities.

GENERAL
▲ Practicality, organization, learning new skills, groundedness.

▼ Impatience, restlessness, lack of focus.

LOVE
▲ New opportunities, practical approach to love, beginning stages of a stable relationship.

▼ Lack of progress, immaturity, distraction from relationship goals.

MONEY
▲ Organization, practicality, learning new financial skills, groundedness.

▼ Impatience, restlessness, impulsive financial decisions, neglecting financial planning.

CAREER
▲ Organization, practicality, learning new skills, reliable approach.

▼ Impatience, restlessness, impulsive decisions, neglecting foundational work.

HEALTH-WELLBEING
▲ Organization, practicality, learning new health routines.

▼ Impatience, restlessness, impulsive decisions, neglecting healthy habits.

SPIRITUALITY
▲ Spiritual curiosity, learning, new skills.

▼ Distraction, lack of focus, spiritual doubt.

COURT CARD | KNIGHT
Symbolize action, adventure, and movement

KNIGHT of PENTACLES.

Knight of Pentacles
"DEPENDABILITY AND METHODICAL PROGRESS"

Depicting a knight on a horse with a pentacle. It symbolizes the reliable and methodical approach to achieving material goals.

Uriel
Archangel

Earth
Element

Root
Chakras

Physical
Domain

Clubs
Traditional Cards

Steady progress, reliability, practicality.
GREEN

Determination, passionate, work ethic
RED

Purity of purpose, meticulous planning.
WHITE

Endurance, discipline, responsibility.
BLACK

HORSE:
Steady and reliable.

FARMLAND AND FIELD:
Productivity and resource management.

MOUNTAINS:
Perseverance in facing challenges.

TREES:
Gradual progress and development.

ARMOR:
Protection and resilience.

GLOVE:
Precision and attention to details.

GREEN PLUME:
Growth and abundance.

GENERAL

▲ Reliability, responsibility, hard work, commitment.

▼ Workaholism, rigidity, being overly cautious.

LOVE

▲ Steadiness, reliability, slow and steady growth in love.

▼ Stagnation, lack of progress, stubbornness.

MONEY

▲ Reliability, responsibility, hard work, commitment, financial stability.

▼ Workaholism, rigidity, over-caution, neglecting emotional aspects of financial decisions.

CAREER

▲ Reliability, responsibility, hard work, commitment, stability in career.

▼ Workaholism, rigidity, over-caution, neglecting emotional aspects of work.

HEALTH-WELLBEING

▲ Reliability, responsibility, hard work, commitment to healthy routines.

▼ Workaholism, rigidity, over-caution, neglecting emotional well-being.

SPIRITUALITY

▲ Spiritual reliability, methodical approach, persistence.

▼ Procrastination, spiritual laziness, lack of commitment.

COURT CARD | QUEEN
Represent nurturing, authority, and intuition.

QUEEN of PENTACLES

Queen of Pentacles
"NURTURING AND PRACTICAL WISDOM"

Features a queen surrounded by nature and holding a pentacle. It symbolizes the ability to nurture and provide practical support in the material realm.

Uriel
Archangel

Earth
Element

Root
Chakras

Physical
Domain

Clubs
Traditional Cards

GREEN	Nurturing, abundance, practical wisdom.
BLUE	Stability, security.
GOLD	Material prosperity, generosity.
RED	Passion for nurturing, warmth, strength.

ROSES:
Beauty and rewards.

THRONE:
Authority and stability.

CHERUBS:
Nurturing and love.

RAM:
Determination and strength.

FLORA:
Connection to nature.

CROWN:
Achievements and mastery.

RABBIT:
Fertility and growth.

GENERAL
▲ Nurturing, practicality, resourcefulness, stability.

▼ Possessiveness, control issues, smothering.

LOVE
▲ Nurturing, practical support, creating a loving home.

▼ Work-life imbalance, neglecting self-care, over-dependency.

MONEY
▲ Nurturing, resourcefulness, practicality, managing finances wisely, providing for others.

▼ Smothering, controlling, neglecting personal financial growth, overspending.

CAREER
▲ Nurturing, resourcefulness, practicality, managing resources wisely, providing for others.

▼ Smothering, controlling, neglecting personal growth, overindulgence.

HEALTH-WELLBEING
▲ Nurturing, resourcefulness, managing health holistically, providing for others.

▼ Smothering, controlling, neglecting personal health needs, overindulgence.

SPIRITUALITY
▲ Nurturing, spiritual abundance, practical wisdom.

▼ Neglect, materialism, lack of focus.

Past or Present

COURT CARD | KING
Symbolize mastery, authority, and control

KING of PENTACLES.

King of Pentacles

"WEALTH AND MASTERY OF THE MATERIAL REALM"

Depicting a king holding a pentacle, it signifies the ability to master and govern material resources.

 Uriel *Archangel*

 Earth *Element*

 Root *Chakras*

 Physical *Domain*

 Clubs *Traditional Cards*

Financial mastery, growth, stability. **GREEN**	Stability, guidance, trustworthiness, dependability. **BLUE**
Wealth, abundance, success. **GOLD**	Passionate leadership, strength, practicality. **RED**

BATTLEMENT:
Secure foundation.

BULLS:
Financial strength.

ARMOR:
Protection and resilience.

CROWN:
Regal authority.

SCEPTER:
Financial rulership.

GRAPES:
Enjoying the rewards.

GENERAL

▲ Success, achievement, security, leadership.

▼ Materialism, greed, neglecting spiritual growth.

LOVE

▲ Stability, security, a dependable partner.

▼ Materialism, possessiveness, controlling behavior.

MONEY

▲ Success, achievement, financial security, providing for family, leadership in financial matters.

▼ Materialism, workaholism, neglecting ethical financial practices, controlling financial decisions.

CAREER

▲ Success, achievement, security, leadership, providing support for others' career growth.

▼ Tyranny, rigidity, controlling behavior, neglecting collaboration, neglecting ethical considerations.

HEALTH-WELLBEING

▲ Achievement, security, providing support for others' health, leadership.

▼ Materialism, workaholism, neglecting ethical healthcare practices, controlling others' health.

SPIRITUALITY

▲ Spiritual mastery, leadership, wisdom.

▼ Greed, tyranny, spiritual arrogance.

Swords

SUIT

Ace of Swords

Two of Swords

Three of Swords

Four of Swords

Five of Swords

Six of Swords

Seven of Swords

Eight of Swords

Nine of Swords

Ten of Swords

Page of Swords

Knight of Swords

Queen of Swords

King of Swords

1 | ACE
Beginnings, potential new opportunities.

Ace of Swords

"CLARITY AND NEW PERSPECTIVES"
Depicting a hand emerging from a cloud holding a sword, it symbolizes the potential for mental clarity and the emergence of new ideas.

Raphael
Archangel

Air
Element

Throat
Chakras

Mental
Domain

Spades
Traditional Cards

Clarity, truth, intellectual insight.	Neutrality, objectivity.	Mental clarity, divine insights, breakthroughs	Mental clarity, objectivity, clear choices.
BLUE	**GREY**	**YELLOW**	**WHITE**

HAND OF GOD:
Divine guidance.

CROWN:
Authority and clarity.

YODS:
Spiritual inspiration.

PALM AND OLIVE BRANCH:
Victory and peace.

BARREN LANDSCAPE:
Need for truth.

GENERAL
▲ New beginnings, clarity, truth, insight.

▼ Confusion, lack of direction, self-deception.

LOVE
▲ Clarity, honest communication, new ideas or perspectives in a relationship.

▼ Miscommunication, confusion, conflict.

MONEY
▲ Clarity, truth, insight leading to sound financial decisions.

▼ Confusion, self-deception, poor financial choices.

CAREER
▲ Clarity, truth, insight leading to clear career direction, new beginnings.

▼ Confusion, self-deception, ignoring important information, unclear goals.

HEALTH-WELLBEING
▲ Clarity, truth, insight leading to healthy choices, new beginnings.

▼ Confusion, self-deception, ignoring health concerns.

SPIRITUALITY
▲ Spiritual clarity, truth, enlightenment.

▼ Confusion, misleading thoughts, mental block.

2 | TWO
Balance, duality, partnerships, choices.

Two of Swords

"DECISION-MAKING AND BALANCE"
Featuring a figure blindfolded with two swords crossed, it symbolizes the need for balanced decision-making and the potential for mental conflict.

Raphael
Archangel

Air
Element

Third Eye
Chakras

Mental
Domain

Spades
Traditional Cards

Intuition, inner balance, decision-making	Uncertainty, impartiality, neutrality.	Mental clarity, objectivity, clear choices.	Blocked emotions, inner conflict, indecision.
BLUE	**SILVER**	**WHITE**	**BLACK**

CROSSED SWORDS:
Decision-making.

BLINDFOLD:
Need for clarity.

CRESCENT MOON:
Emotions in play.

SEA:
Depth of emotions.

ROCKS:
Challenges to navigate.

BENCH:
Temporary pause.

GENERAL
▲ Balance, justice, fairness, making tough choices.

▼ Imbalance, indecision, unfair treatment.

LOVE
▲ Indecision, stalemate, needing to make a choice in love.

▼ Clarity, making a decision, overcoming avoidance.

MONEY
▲ Balance, fairness, making tough financial choices.

▼ Imbalance, unfair treatment, neglecting ethical business practices.

CAREER
▲ Balance, fairness, making tough career decisions, weighing options.

▼ Imbalance, unfair treatment, struggling to make decisions, procrastination.

HEALTH-WELLBEING
▲ Balance, fairness, making tough health decisions.

▼ Imbalance, unfair treatment, neglecting mental health needs.

SPIRITUALITY
▲ Spiritual decision, balance, inner peace.

▼ Indecision, stalemate, disconnection.

3 | THREE
Growth, creativity, collaboration.

Three of Swords

"HEARTBREAK AND EMOTIONAL PAIN"
Depicting three swords piercing a heart, it symbolizes the experience of emotional suffering and the need for healing.

Raphael
Archangel

Air
Element

Heart
Chakras

Mental
Domain

Spades
Traditional Cards

Sorrow, detachment, neutrality.
GREY

Heartbreak, pain, emotional turmoil.
RED

Grief, loss, deep emotional wounds.
BLACK

Healing, acceptance, clarity after pain.
WHITE

PIERCED HEART:
Deep emotional pain.

NO PEOPLE:
Personal suffering.

THUNDER:
Sudden disruptive force.

RAIN:
Symbol of tears.

CLOUDS:
Dark and somber mood.

GENERAL
▲ Grief, loss, heartbreak, betrayal.

▼ Acceptance, moving on, healing.

LOVE
▲ Heartbreak, sorrow, emotional pain.

▼ Healing from heartbreak, releasing pain, forgiveness.

MONEY
▲ Loss, grief, financial hardship, emotional impact.

▼ Acceptance, moving on, learning from financial mistakes.

CAREER
▲ Loss, grief, facing career challenges, emotional impact.

▼ Acceptance, learning from setbacks, moving forward with resilience.

HEALTH-WELLBEING
▲ Loss, grief, facing health challenges, emotional impact.

▼ Acceptance, moving on, learning from illness.

SPIRITUALITY
▲ Heartbreak, emotional pain, spiritual growth.

▼ Healing, recovery, emotional release.

4 | FOUR
Stability, structure, foundation.

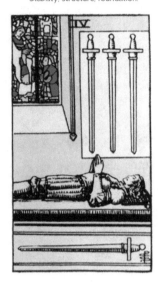

Four of Swords

"REST AND CONTEMPLATION"
Featuring a figure resting with four swords above, it symbolizes the need for mental recuperation and a period of contemplative rest.

Raphael	**Air**	**Third Eye**	**Mental**	**Spades**
Archangel	*Element*	*Chakras*	*Domain*	*Traditional Cards*

BLUE	YELLOW	PURPLE	GREY
Rest, tranquility, mental peace.	Mental clarity and focus, healing process.	Spiritual healing, meditation, inner reflection.	Quiet contemplation, solitude, mental stillness.

TOMB:
Rest and recovery.

STAINED-GLASS WINDOW:
Spiritual connection.

ARMOR:
Protection and readiness.

HANGING SWORDS:
Temporary mental pause.

GENERAL
▲ Rest, reflection, introspection, peace of mind.

▼ Stagnation, avoidance, fear of facing reality.

LOVE
▲ Rest, recovery, taking a break from a relationship.

▼ Restlessness, needing to take action, burnout.

MONEY
▲ Rest, reflection, introspection, time for financial planning.

▼ Avoidance, fear of facing financial reality, procrastination.

CAREER
▲ Rest, reflection, introspection, time for career planning.

▼ Avoidance, fear of facing challenges, procrastination, neglecting responsibilities.

HEALTH-WELLBEING
▲ Rest, reflection, introspection, time for healing.

▼ Avoidance, fear of facing health concerns, procrastination.

SPIRITUALITY
▲ Spiritual rest, contemplation, renewal.

▼ Restlessness, exhaustion, neglecting spirituality.

5 | FIVE
Change, conflict, instability, challenge

Five of Swords

"CONFLICT AND UNREST"

Featuring a figure holding three swords triumphantly and two figures in the background, it symbolizes the aftermath of a conflict and the potential for resentment.

 Raphael
Archangel

 Air
Element

Throat
Chakras

 Mental
Domain

 Spades
Traditional Cards

Defeat, detachment, neutrality.	Conflict, aggression, challenges.
GREY	**RED**

Betrayal, loss, negative outcomes..	Deceptive strategies, manipulation, trickery, rivalry.
BLACK	**GREEN**

SMILING CHAMPION:
Questionable victory.

STORMY SKY:
Turbulent environment.

CLOUDS:
Discord and confusion.

MOUNTAINS:
Overcoming challenges at a cost.

SEA:
Emotional aftermath.

GENERAL
▲ Defeat, surrender, loss, feeling overwhelmed.

▼ Hitting rock bottom, finding new strength, self-discovery.

LOVE
▲ Conflict, betrayal, tension in a relationship.

▼ Resolution, moving past conflicts, making amends.

MONEY
▲ Defeat, surrender, financial loss, hitting rock bottom.

▼ Finding new strength, starting over, learning from setbacks.

CAREER
▲ Defeat, surrender, hitting rock bottom, accepting limitations.

▼ Finding new strength, starting over, learning from career setbacks.

HEALTH-WELLBEING
▲ Defeat, surrender, hitting rock bottom, accepting limitations.

▼ Finding new strength, starting over, learning from health setbacks.

SPIRITUALITY
▲ Spiritual conflict, tension, ego struggle.

▼ Resolution, reconciliation, inner peace.

6 | SIX
Harmony, balance, resolution.

Six of Swords

"TRANSITION AND MOVING ON"

Featuring a figure in a boat being ferried across water, it symbolizes the journey from troubled waters to calmer shores and the pursuit of mental peace.

Raphael
Archangel

Air
Element

Throat
Chakras

Mental
Domain

Spades
Traditional Cards

Transition, mental clarity, calm waters.
BLUE

Transition, neutrality, moving forward.
GREY

Determination, difficult past to a more stable future.
RED

Spiritual transition, transformation, healing, intuitive navigation.
PURPLE

FERRYMAN:
Guiding transition.

UPRIGHT SWORDS:
Mental shift.

BOAT:
Journey from difficulties.

SEA:
Emotional navigation.

TREES:
Promise of peace.

GENERAL
▲ Recovery, healing, moving forward, letting go.

▼ Reluctance to let go, clinging to the past, fear of change.

LOVE
▲ Moving on, healing journeys, transitioning to better times in love.

▼ Resistance to change, unresolved issues, feeling stuck.

MONEY
▲ Recovery, healing, moving forward, overcoming financial hardship.

▼ Reluctance to let go, clinging to past losses, fear of moving on.

CAREER
▲ Recovery, healing, moving forward after career challenges, overcoming obstacles.

▼ Reluctance to let go, clinging to past failures, fear of moving on.

HEALTH-WELLBEING
▲ Recovery, healing, moving forward, overcoming illness.

▼ Reluctance to let go, clinging to past health issues, fear of moving on.

SPIRITUALITY
▲ Transition, spiritual journey, moving forward.

▼ Stagnation, fear of change, incomplete transition.

7 | SEVEN
Strategy, introspection, reflection, spirituality

Seven of Swords

"DECEPTION AND STRATEGY"

Depicting a figure carrying five swords away, it symbolizes the themes of deception, strategic thinking, and the need for caution in the intellectual realm.

Raphael *Archangel*	**Air** *Element*	**Third Eye** *Chakras*	**Mental** *Domain*	**Spades** *Traditional Cards*

YELLOW	GREY	BLUE	RED
Caution, vigilance, awareness.	Secrecy, stealth, hidden motives.	Deception, hidden truths, mental strategies.	Cunning strategies, manipulation.

THIEF:
Deceptive actions.

RED FEZ HAT:
Clandestine behavior.

YELLOW SKY:
Caution and warning.

HOLDING SHARP END OF SWORDS:
Calculated and possibly dishonest approach.

GENERAL

▲ Deception, betrayal, hidden agendas, trickery.

▼ Facing deception, uncovering truth, self-defense.

LOVE

▲ Deception, secretiveness, betrayal in a relationship.

▼ Coming clean, honesty, overcoming deceit.

MONEY

▲ Deception, hidden agendas, trickery, uncovering financial secrets.

▼ Facing deception, setting boundaries, protecting your assets.

CAREER

▲ Deception, hidden agendas, discovering career manipulations, facing truth.

▼ Facing deception head-on, setting boundaries, protecting your career interests.

HEALTH-WELLBEING

▲ Deception, hidden agendas, discovering health concerns, facing truth.

▼ Facing deception, setting boundaries, protecting your health.

SPIRITUALITY

▲ Deception, strategic thinking, spiritual stealth.

▼ Honesty, spiritual exposure, truth revealed.

8 | EIGHT
Power, progress, movement.

Eight of Swords

"CONFINEMENT AND SELF-IMPOSED RESTRICTIONS"
Depicting a figure blindfolded and bound, surrounded by eight swords, it symbolizes the mental challenges that arise from limiting beliefs and self-imposed constraints.

Raphael
Archangel

Air
Element

Third Eye
Chakras

Mental
Domain

Spades
Traditional Cards

Mental clarity, communication, breaking free.
BLUE

Restriction, feeling trapped, mental confusion.
GREY

Fear, restriction, feeling powerless.
BLACK

Urgency, trapped emotions, inner turmoil.
RED

ROPES:
Self-imposed restrictions.

BLINDFOLD:
Lack of awareness.

UPRIGHT SWORDS:
Mental entrapment.

CLIFF:
Perceived barrier.

CASTLE:
Unreachable refuge.

SEA:
Depth of emotional impact.

GENERAL
▲ Communication, movement, quick thinking, adaptability.

▼ Gossip, rumors, scattered thoughts, communication breakdown.

LOVE
▲ Feeling trapped, anxiety, limitations in love.

▼ Release, gaining perspective, overcoming obstacles.

MONEY
▲ Communication, quick thinking, adapting to financial fluctuations.

▼ Gossip, rumors, scattered thoughts, communication breakdown.

CAREER
▲ Communication, quick thinking, adapting to career changes, overcoming limitations.

▼ Scattered thoughts, communication breakdowns, feeling stuck, neglecting important conversations.

HEALTH-WELLBEING
▲ Communication, quick thinking, adapting to health changes.

▼ Gossip, rumors, scattered thoughts, communication breakdown impacting health.

SPIRITUALITY
▲ Spiritual restrictions, feeling stuck, self-imposed limitations.

▼ Liberation, new perspectives, breaking free.

9 | NINE
Fulfillment, nearing completion, introspection.

Nine of Swords

"ANXIETY AND MENTAL TURMOIL"
Featuring a figure in bed with nine swords hanging over, it symbolizes the impact of overwhelming thoughts and the need for addressing mental distress.

Raphael	**Air**	**Third Eye**	**Mental**	**Spades**
Archangel	*Element*	*Chakras*	*Domain*	*Traditional Cards*

BLACK	BLUE	RED	PINK
Anxiety, nightmares, deep fears.	Mental anguish, communication of fears.	Emotional turmoil, stress, restlessness.	Seeking emotional support, emotional vulnerability.

HANGING SWORDS:
Mental distress.

HANDS OVER EYES:
Avoidance and helplessness.

BEDSPREAD:
Restless nights.

ROSES:
Beauty amidst pain.

BED CARVINGS:
Internal struggles.

GENERAL
▲ Cruelty, aggression, conflict, mental anguish.

▼ Overcoming fear, inner strength, setting boundaries.

LOVE
▲ Anxiety, worry, sleepless nights over relationship issues.

▼ Overcoming anxiety, finding peace, resolving fears.

MONEY
▲ Cruelty, emotional pain, arguments, legal disputes.

▼ Setting boundaries, finding strength, ending unhealthy financial partnerships.

CAREER
▲ Cruelty, emotional pain, arguments, legal disputes impacting career.

▼ Setting boundaries, finding strength, ending unhealthy career connections.

HEALTH-WELLBEING
▲ Cruelty, emotional pain, arguments, legal disputes impacting health.

▼ Setting boundaries, finding strength, ending unhealthy relationships.

SPIRITUALITY
▲ Spiritual anxiety, guilt, inner turmoil.

▼ Release of anxiety, inner peace, healing.

10 | TEN
Completion, culmination, new cycles.

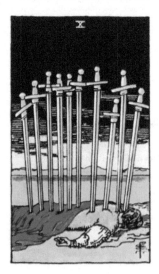

Ten of Swords

"ENDINGS AND NEW BEGINNINGS"
Depicting a figure lying beneath ten swords, it symbolizes the completion of a challenging mental cycle and the potential for new beginnings.

Raphael
Archangel

Air
Element

Throat
Chakras

Mental
Domain

Spades
Traditional Cards

Painful transition, crisis, transformation.	Endings, deep wounds, surrender.	Potential for gaining valuable insights	Mental clarity, communication of pain, healing thoughts.
RED	**BLACK**	**YELLOW**	**BLUE**

DEAD OR ALIVE?:
Symbolic ending.

CHAKRA ALIGNMENT:
Energy transformation.

HAND GESTURE:
Surrender or acceptance.

SKY:
Turbulent emotions.

SEA:
Profound emotional impact.

MOUNTAINS:
Overcoming obstacles..

GENERAL
▲ Ruin, destruction, endings, sudden change.

▼ Transformation, rebirth, letting go of the past.

LOVE
▲ Endings, betrayal, hitting rock bottom.

▼ Recovery, regeneration, surviving a difficult period.

MONEY
▲ Ruin, sudden change, unexpected financial losses, transformation.

▼ Personal growth, liberation, letting go of unhealthy financial patterns.

CAREER
▲ Ruin, sudden change, unexpected career challenges, transformation.

▼ Personal growth, liberation, letting go of unhealthy career situations, new opportunities.

HEALTH-WELLBEING
▲ Ruin, sudden change, unexpected health issues, transformation.

▼ Personal growth, liberation, letting go of unhealthy habits.

SPIRITUALITY
▲ Spiritual endings, transformation, acceptance.

▼ Recovery, rebirth, overcoming trauma.

COURT CARD | PAGE
Represent beginnings, learning, and messages.

PAGE of SWORDS.

Page of Swords

"CURIOSITY AND VIGILANCE"
Features a young figure holding a sword with a keen expression. It symbolizes the inquisitive nature and the eagerness to explore new ideas.

Raphael	**Air**	**Throat**	**Mental**	**Spades**
Archangel	*Element*	*Chakras*	*Domain*	*Traditional Cards*

BLUE — Clarity of thought, logic

YELLOW — Intellectual agility, optimism.

RED — Determination, assertiveness, swift action

PINK — Curiosity, compassion.

SWORD IN LEFT HAND:
Intuitive approach.

FOREGROUND:
Attentiveness and readiness.

MOUNTAINS:
Overcoming obstacles.

BIRDS:
Sharp and alert mind.

GREEN FEATHER:
Openness to learning.

GENERAL
▲ Curiosity, intellect, seeking knowledge, communication.

▼ Gossip, criticism, shallow thinking.

LOVE
▲ Curiosity, new communication, mental agility in love.

▼ Gossip, miscommunication, immature behavior.

MONEY
▲ Curiosity, intellectual approach, research, critical thinking.

▼ Criticism, gossip, shallowness, impulsive financial decisions.

CAREER
▲ Curiosity, intellectual approach, researching career options, eagerness to learn.

▼ Criticism, gossip, shallowness, impulsive career decisions.

HEALTH-WELLBEING
▲ Curiosity, intellectual approach, researching health information.

▼ Criticism, gossip, shallowness, impulsive health decisions.

SPIRITUALITY
▲ Spiritual curiosity, new ideas, seeking truth.

▼ Hasty decisions, lack of focus, impulsiveness.

COURT CARD | KNIGHT
Symbolize action, adventure, and movement.

KNIGHT of SWORDS .

Knight of Swords
"AMBITION AND ASSERTIVENESS"

Depicting a knight charging forward with a raised sword, it symbolizes the determination to pursue goals and the assertive nature of the knight.

| Raphael *Archangel* | Air *Element* | Throat *Chakras* | Mental *Domain* | Spades *Traditional Cards* |

| | Analytical approach, impartiality. | | Clarity of thought, logic. | | Determination, assertiveness, swift action. | | Intellectual precision, mental clarity, sharp focus, confidence. |
| **GREY** | | **BLUE** | | **RED** | | **YELLOW** |

WHITE HORSE:
Purity and speed.

YELLOW BUTTERFLIES:
Transformation.

FALCON:
Keen vision and focus.

BIRDS:
Swift navigation.

RED GLOVE:
Passion and assertiveness.

TREES:
Overcoming obstacles.

SKY:
Limitless possibilities.

GENERAL

▲ Power, courage, action, taking initiative.

▼ Aggression, impulsiveness, recklessness.

LOVE

▲ Swift action, direct communication, boldness in love.

▼ Impulsiveness, recklessness, harsh words.

MONEY

▲ Action, taking initiative, directness, making quick financial decisions.

▼ Aggression, impulsiveness, rushing into investments.

CAREER

▲ Action, taking initiative, directness, making quick career decisions.

▼ Aggression, impulsiveness, rushing into projects, neglecting planning.

HEALTH-WELLBEING

▲ Action, taking initiative, directness, making quick health decisions.

▼ Aggression, impulsiveness, rushing into treatment, neglecting medical advice.

SPIRITUALITY

▲ Spiritual ambition, quick thinking, determination.

▼ Aggression, impatience, lack of control.

COURT CARD | QUEEN
Represent nurturing, authority, and intuition.

SWORD IN RIGHT HAND:
Clear and decisive thinking.

YELLOW BUTTERFLIES:
Thoughtful adaptation.

CHERUB:
Connection to
higher wisdom.

CROWN:
Authority and wisdom.

RED VEIL:
Warmth and depth
of emotion.

STORM CLOUDS:
Resilience in
facing challenges.

Queen of Swords

"INDEPENDENCE AND WISDOM"
Features a queen holding a sword with a stern expression. It symbolizes the ability to make decisions with clarity, independence, and a sharp intellect.

Raphael
Archangel

Air
Element

Throat
Chakras

Mental
Domain

Spades
Traditional Cards

Clear communication, intellectual insight.	Detachment, impartiality, analytical thinking.	Passionate pursuit of truth and justice.	Clarity, objectivity, rationality.
BLUE	**GREY**	**RED**	**YELLOW**

GENERAL
▲ Intelligence, discernment, independence, clarity.

▼ Harshness, coldness, emotional unavailability.

LOVE
▲ Independence, clear boundaries, wisdom in relationships.

▼ Coldness, bitterness, overly critical.

MONEY
▲ Intelligence, discernment, independence, clear financial strategies.

▼ Harshness, coldness, neglecting emotional aspects of financial decisions.

CAREER
▲ Intelligence, discernment, independence, clear strategies for career success.

▼ Harshness, coldness, neglecting emotional aspects of career, neglecting self-care.

HEALTH-WELLBEING
▲ Intelligence, discernment, independence, clear strategies for health.

▼ Harshness, coldness, neglecting emotional aspects of health, neglecting self-care.

SPIRITUALITY
▲ Spiritual wisdom, clarity, independence.

▼ Harshness, spiritual coldness, disconnection.

COURT CARD | KING
Symbolize mastery, authority, and control.

KING of SWORDS.

King of Swords

"AUTHORITY AND MENTAL CLARITY"
Depicting a king with a raised sword, it symbolizes the mastery of intellect, clear communication, and the authoritative nature of the king.

 Raphael *Archangel*

 Air *Element*

 Throat *Chakras*

 Mental *Domain*

 Spades *Traditional Cards*

Clear communication, logic. **BLUE**	Authority, mastery, and the masculine energy of the sun. **GOLD**
Wisdom, objectivity, fairness. **WHITE**	Assertive leadership, strategic thinking. **RED**

SWORD:
Authority and clear thinking.

THRONE:
Leadership and intellect.

BUTTERFLY:
Adaptability and transformation.

MOON:
Intuition and subconscious awareness.

NYMPHS:
Harmony with nature and creativity.

BIRDS:
Effective communication of ideas.

TREES AND CLOUDS:
Balancing practicality and abstract thought.

GENERAL
▲ Justice, fairness, authority, leadership.

▼ Tyranny, rigidity, abuse of power.

LOVE
▲ Logic, authority, intellectual approach to love.

▼ Manipulation, tyranny, lack of empathy.

MONEY
▲ Justice, fairness, responsibility, ethical financial practices.

▼ Tyranny, rigidity, controlling finances, unethical practices.

CAREER
▲ Justice, fairness, responsibility, ethical career practices, leadership.

▼ Tyranny, rigidity, controlling behavior, neglecting collaboration, neglecting ethical considerations.

HEALTH-WELLBEING
▲ Justice, fairness, responsibility, ethical healthcare practices.

▼ Tyranny, rigidity, controlling treatment decisions, neglecting holistic approach.

SPIRITUALITY
▲ Spiritual authority, intellectual power, leadership.

▼ Tyranny, manipulation, abuse of power.

Wands

SUIT

Ace of Wands

Two of Wands

Three of Wands

Four of Wands

Five of Wands

Six of Wands

Seven of Wands

Eight of Wands

Nine of Wands

Ten of Wands

Page of Wands

Knight of Wands

Queen of Wands

King of Wands

1 | ACE
Beginnings, potential, new opportunities.

ACE of WANDS.

Ace of Wands

"SPARK OF INSPIRATION AND NEW BEGINNINGS"
Depicting a hand holding a wand with leaves sprouting, it symbolizes the pure energy of potential and creative force.

Michael
Archangel

Fire
Element

Plexus
Chakras

Spiritual
Domain

Diamonds
Traditional Cards

Inspiration, optimism, clarity.	Growth, potential, and abundance.	Passion, energy, creative force.	Communication, clarity, and truth.
YELLOW	**GREEN**	**RED**	**BLUE**

WAND:
Creative potential.

HAND:
Active intention.

CLOUDS:
Limitless possibilities.

LEAVES:
Growth and vitality.

YODS:
Divine inspiration.

RIVER:
Fluid creativity.

CASTLE:
Achievement and success.

GENERAL
▲ New beginnings, inspiration, creativity, passion.

▼ Stagnation, lack of motivation, blocked creativity.

LOVE
▲ New beginnings, passionate energy, exciting new romance.

▼ Delays, lack of motivation, missed opportunities in love.

MONEY
▲ New beginnings, financial opportunities, inspiration, investments.

▼ Stagnation, lack of opportunity, blocked creativity.

CAREER
▲ New beginnings, inspiration, creative spark, taking action towards career goals.

▼ Stagnation, lack of motivation, neglecting creative impulses, blocked opportunities.

HEALTH-WELLBEING
▲ New beginnings, inspiration, energy boost, taking action for health.

▼ Stagnation, lack of motivation, neglecting health, blocked creativity.

SPIRITUALITY
▲ Spiritual inspiration, passion, creativity.

▼ Lack of inspiration, blocked creativity, delay.

2 | TWO
Balance, duality, partnerships, choices.

CASTLE:
Stability and power.

GLOBE:
Global awareness
and expansion.

FLOWERS:
Growth and beauty.

SEA:
Vast opportunities.

FOREST:
Untapped resources.

MOUNTAINS:
Potential challenges.

Two of Wands

"PLANNING AND PERSONAL POWER"
Featuring a figure holding a globe and wand, it symbolizes the exploration
of possibilities and asserting one's influence on the world.

Michael	**Fire**	**Plexus**	**Spiritual**	**Diamonds**
Archangel	*Element*	*Chakras*	*Domain*	*Traditional Cards*

Ambition, boldness, taking charge.	Planning, decision-making, confidence	Growth, balance, choices.	Vision, foresight, future possibilities.
RED	**YELLOW**	**GREEN**	**BLUE**

GENERAL
▲ Duality, conflict, choices, taking action.

▼ Indecision, missed opportunities, internal conflict.

LOVE
▲ Planning for the future, making decisions together, partnership.

▼ Indecision, fear of change, lack of direction.

MONEY
▲ Balancing finances, budgeting, adaptation, juggling resources.

▼ Uncertainty, instability, feeling overwhelmed.

CAREER
▲ Planning, strategizing, exploring career options, considering different paths.

▼ Indecision, scattered energy, neglecting focused action, lacking clear direction.

HEALTH-WELLBEING
▲ Duality, choices, finding balance, work-life balance impacting health.

▼ Indecision, stress, neglecting one aspect of health (physical/mental/emotional).

SPIRITUALITY
▲ Spiritual planning, vision, direction.

▼ Indecision, lack of direction, hesitance.

3 | THREE
Growth, creativity, collaboration.

Three of Wands

"EXPANSION AND EXPLORATION"
Depicting a figure overlooking the horizon with three wands, it symbolizes the anticipation of growth and the exploration of new horizons.

Michael
Archangel

Fire
Element

Plexus
Chakras

Spiritual
Domain

Diamonds
Traditional Cards

YELLOW	GREEN	RED	BLUE
Expansion, optimism, foresight.	Growth, abundance, prosperity.	Enterprise, leadership, taking action.	Exploration, planning, broad perspective.

MAN:
Stands for looking forward confidently.

WANDS:
Represent stability and support.

LANDSCAPE:
Symbolizes opportunities and potential.

CLOTHING:
Reflects optimism and energy.

SHIPS:
Indicate outcomes and results.

GENERAL
▲ Communication, exploration, travel, expansion.

▼ Miscommunication, delays, feeling lost.

LOVE
▲ Expansion, long-term vision, waiting for results in a relationship.

▼ Delays, obstacles, frustration in love.

MONEY
▲ Collaboration, teamwork, skilled work, earning potential.

▼ Lack of direction, feeling undervalued, procrastination.

CAREER
▲ Communication, exploration, networking, travel impacting career.

▼ Miscommunication, confusion, neglecting valuable connections, overlooking foreign opportunities.

HEALTH-WELLBEING
▲ Communication, exploration, trying new health practices, travel impacting health.

▼ Miscommunication, confusion, neglecting healthy communication about health.

SPIRITUALITY
▲ Spiritual expansion, progress, broader vision.

▼ Stagnation, delays, limited outlook.

4 | FOUR
Stability, structure, foundation

Four of Wands

"CELEBRATION AND STABILITY"
Depicting figures holding wands in a celebratory arch, it symbolizes the achievement of a milestone and the establishment of a solid foundation.

Michael	Fire	Heart	Spiritual	Diamonds
Archangel	*Element*	*Chakras*	*Domain*	*Traditional Cards*

YELLOW	GREEN	RED	BLUE
Happiness, optimism, community	Harmony, stability, growth.	Celebration, passion, joy.	Tranquility, balance, unity

ARCHWAY:
Passage to celebration.

FLOWERS:
Beauty and growth.

GRAPEVINE:
Prosperity and abundance.

CASTLE:
Stability and accomplishment.

MOAT:
Protection and security.

BRIDGE:
Transition to a harmonious phase.

YELLOW SKY:
Optimism and joy.

GENERAL

▲ Stability, foundation, planning, hard work.

▼ Stagnation, boredom, lack of progress.

LOVE

▲ Celebration, harmony, marriage, stable relationship.

▼ Conflict, instability, feeling unwelcome.

MONEY

▲ Stability, secure foundation, long-term planning, careful spending.

▼ Stagnation, lack of progress, boredom.

CAREER

▲ Stability, foundation, secure work environment, finding your niche.

▼ Stagnation, boredom, fear of change, resisting necessary growth .

HEALTH-WELLBEING

▲ Stability, foundation, routine, healthy habits.

▼ Stagnation, boredom, neglecting exercise, unhealthy routines.

SPIRITUALITY

▲ Spiritual stability, community, harmony.

▼ Discord, instability, lack of harmony.

5 | FIVE
Change, conflict, instability, challenge

Five of Wands

"COMPETITION AND CONFLICT"
Featuring figures engaged in a dynamic struggle with wands, it symbolizes the challenges that arise in competitive situations.

Michael	**Fire**	**Plexus**	**Spiritual**	**Diamonds**
Archangel	*Element*	*Chakras*	*Domain*	*Traditional Cards*

RED	YELLOW	BROWN	BLUE
Conflict, competition, energy.	Individuality, assertiveness, competition.	Stability, grounding, finding common ground.	Communication, understanding, resolution.

BATTLE:
Conflict and competition.

BLUE SKY:
Potential for resolution.

BARREN LANDSCAPE:
Unproductive challenges.

GENERAL
▲ Conflict, competition, challenges, unexpected changes.

▼ Overcoming obstacles, resilience, finding strength.

LOVE
▲ Conflict, competition, disagreements.

▼ Resolution, avoiding conflict, finding common ground.

MONEY
▲ Loss, setbacks, unexpected expenses, financial challenges.

▼ Overcoming obstacles, resilience, resourcefulness.

CAREER
▲ Healthy competition, overcoming challenges, navigating conflict constructively.

▼ Unhealthy competition, burnout, feeling overwhelmed, losing sight of the goal.

HEALTH-WELLBEING
▲ Conflict, challenges, overcoming obstacles, illness.

▼ Resilience, finding strength, learning from setbacks.

SPIRITUALITY
▲ Spiritual competition, conflict, challenge.

▼ Resolution, harmony, avoiding conflict.

6 | SIX
Harmony, balance, resolution.

Six of Wands

"VICTORY AND RECOGNITION"
Depicting a figure riding a horse with a wand held high, it symbolizes the attainment of success and public acknowledgment.

Michael	**Fire**	**Plexus**	**Spiritual**	**Diamonds**
Archangel	*Element*	*Chakras*	*Domain*	*Traditional Cards*

Triumph, success, recognition.	Confidence, optimism, public acclaim.	Growth, harmony, validation.	Communication, leadership, victory.
RED	**YELLOW**	**GREEN**	**BLUE**

HORSEMAN:
Triumph and success.

LAUREL WREATHS:
Honor and recognition.

HORSE:
Strength and support.

GAUNTLET GLOVES:
Conquering challenges.

RIBBON:
Unity and celebration.

GENERAL
▲ Victory, success, recognition, overcoming challenges.

▼ Unearned rewards, self-doubt, lack of accomplishment.

LOVE
▲ Success, recognition, achieving goals together.

▼ Lack of recognition, feeling unappreciated, setbacks.

MONEY
▲ Recognition, rewards, success, reaping benefits.

▼ Unearned rewards, superficiality, neglecting financial goals.

CAREER
▲ Recognition, achievement, reaping rewards of hard work, public acknowledgement.

▼ Unearned recognition, superficial success, neglecting team contributions, overlooking potential problems.

HEALTH-WELLBEING
▲ Recognition, rewards, recovery, reaping benefits of healthy choices.

▼ Unearned rewards, superficiality, neglecting long-term health goals.

SPIRITUALITY
▲ Spiritual victory, success, recognition.

▼ Setbacks, pride, loss of confidence.

Current Situation

7 | SEVEN
Strategy, introspection, reflection, spirituality.

Seven of Wands

"COURAGE AND DEFENDING BELIEFS"
Featuring a figure standing on higher ground, warding off others with a wand, it symbolizes the strength to defend personal convictions.

Michael
Archangel

Fire
Element

Plexus
Chakras

Spiritual
Domain

Diamonds
Traditional Cards

Courage, resilience, determination.	Confidence, assertiveness, standing out.
RED	**YELLOW**
Strength, growth, standing one's ground.	Communication, defense, self-expression.
GREEN	**BLUE**

ATTACKERS:
Facing challenges.

MISMATCHED SHOES:
Adaptability.

GREEN TUNIC:
Resilience and growth.

MOUNTAIN SUMMIT:
Elevated perspective.

GENERAL
▲ Courage, perseverance, taking risks, determination.

▼ Recklessness, impulsiveness, giving up easily.

LOVE
▲ Defense, standing your ground, overcoming challenges.

▼ Feeling overwhelmed, giving up, lack of confidence.

MONEY
▲ Taking risks, quick decisions, adaptability, unexpected income.

▼ Recklessness, impulsiveness, gambling, scattered finances.

CAREER
▲ Adaptability, quick thinking, resourcefulness, overcoming unexpected obstacles.

▼ Impulsiveness, recklessness, taking unnecessary risks, neglecting strategic planning.

HEALTH-WELLBEING
▲ Taking risks, adaptability, quick thinking, managing health emergencies.

▼ Recklessness, impulsiveness, neglecting preventative care.

SPIRITUALITY
▲ Spiritual resilience, courage, defense.

▼ Overwhelmed, surrender, loss of courage.

8 | EIGHT
Power, progress, movement.

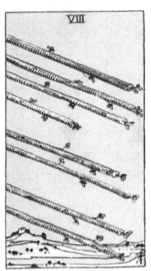

Eight of Wands

"SWIFT ACTION AND MOVEMENT"
Depicting wands in flight, it symbolizes the acceleration of plans and the swift progression of events.

Michael
Archangel

Fire
Element

Plexus
Chakras

Spiritual
Domain

Diamonds
Traditional Cards

Communication, travel, expansion.

BLUE

Growth, energetic flow, rapid movement.

GREEN

Rapid progress, optimism, dynamic energy.

YELLOW

Swift action, energy, movement.

RED

NO PEOPLE:
Emphasis on energy.

DIRECTION OF WANDS:
Rapid movement.

RIVER:
Flow of emotions and energy.

HILLS:
Overcoming challenges swiftly.

CASTLE:
Reaching goals with speed.

GENERAL
▲ Swift action, movement, adaptability, change.

▼ Hastiness, impulsiveness, scattered energy.

LOVE
▲ Swift action, communication, rapid progress in love

▼ Delays, misunderstandings, frustration.

MONEY
▲ Communication, movement, quick thinking, adapting to financial changes.

▼ Gossip, rumors, scattered thoughts, poor communication.

CAREER
▲ Movement, communication, rapid changes, adapting to new career developments.

▼ Scattered energy, communication breakdowns, missing important details, rushing into decisions.

HEALTH-WELLBEING
▲ Movement, communication, quick changes, adapting to health changes.

▼ Scattered energy, communication breakdowns, neglecting doctor's advice.

SPIRITUALITY
▲ Spiritual momentum, movement, swift progress.

▼ Delays, confusion, miscommunication.

9 | NINE
Fulfillment, nearing completion, introspection.

Nine of Wands

"RESILIENCE AND PERSEVERANCE"
Featuring a figure with bandaged head, standing guard with wands in the background, it symbolizes the strength to endure challenges and keep moving forward.

Michael *Archangel* · **Fire** *Element* · **Plexus** *Chakras* · **Spiritual** *Domain* · **Diamonds** *Traditional Cards*

RED — Resilience, strength, determination.

YELLOW — Caution, perseverance, self-preservation.

GREEN — Healing, growth, perseverance.

BLUE — Communication, defense, maintaining boundaries.

UPRIGHT WANDS: Preparedness and determination.

HILLS: Symbol of past challenges.

WHITE BANDAGE: Resilience and healing.

YELLOW BOOTS: Optimism and proactive approach.

GENERAL
▲ Hope, optimism, anticipation, positive outcome.
▼ Disappointment, pessimism, setbacks.

LOVE
▲ Resilience, persistence, maintaining boundaries.
▼ Exhaustion, feeling defensive, lack of support.

MONEY
▲ Hope, optimism, positive outlook, potential prosperity.
▼ Disappointment, pessimism, unrealistic expectations.

CAREER
▲ Perseverance, resilience, overcoming long-term challenges, maintaining hope.
▼ Discouragement, giving up easily, neglecting self-belief, doubting your abilities.

HEALTH-WELLBEING
▲ Hope, optimism, positive outlook, potential for healing.
▼ Disappointment, pessimism, neglecting mental health.

SPIRITUALITY
▲ Spiritual perseverance, endurance, courage.
▼ Fatigue, burnout, giving up.

10 | TEN
Completion, culmination, new cycles.

Ten of Wands

"BURDENS AND RESPONSIBILITIES"
Depicting a figure carrying a heavy bundle of wands, it symbolizes the weight of responsibilities and the challenges of managing multiple tasks.

Michael *Archangel*	**Fire** *Element*	**Plexus** *Chakras*	**Spiritual** *Domain*	**Diamonds** *Traditional Cards*

Burden, pressure, determination.	Optimism, perseverance, reaching a goal.	Communication, expressing burdens.	Energy, enthusiasm, completion of a cycle.
RED	**YELLOW**	**BLUE**	**ORANGE**

MAN BENT OVER:
Symbolizes the weight of responsibilities.

TREES:
Represent obstacles and challenges.

CASTLE:
Distant goal or achievement, hindered by the heavy burden.

GENERAL
▲ Completion, culmination, achievement, fulfillment.

▼ Missed opportunities, limitations, unfulfilled desires.

LOVE
▲ Burden, responsibility, feeling weighed down.

▼ Release of burdens, delegating, avoiding burnout.

MONEY
▲ Completion, culmination, achievement, financial goals met.

▼ Missed opportunities, limitations, feeling unfulfilled.

CAREER
▲ Completion, culmination of efforts, achieving major career goals, feeling overwhelmed.

▼ Missed opportunities, feeling stuck, neglecting self-care, burden of success.

HEALTH-WELLBEING
▲ Completion, culmination, achievement of health goals, self-care.

▼ Missed opportunities, limitations, neglecting long-term goals.

SPIRITUALITY
▲ Spiritual burden, responsibility, hard work.

▼ Release, letting go, lightening the load.

COURT CARD | PAGE
Represent beginnings, learning, and messages.

PAGE of WANDS.

Page of Wands

"CREATIVE EXPLORATION AND PASSIONATE BEGINNINGS"
Depicting a figure holding a wand with a sprouting plant, it symbolizes the potential for creative inspiration and the initiation of passionate endeavors.

| **Michael** *Archangel* | **Fire** *Element* | **Plexus** *Chakras* | **Spiritual** *Domain* | **Diamonds** *Traditional Cards* |

 Enthusiasm, creativity, passion.
RED

 Playfulness, spontaneity, creative projects.
ORANGE

 Curiosity, learning, exploration.
YELLOW

 Communication, expressing ideas, enthusiasm.
BLUE

RED FEATHER:
Signifies passion and creativity.

EXPLORER'S HAT:
Represents curiosity and adventure.

SALAMANDERS:
Symbolizes resilience and transformation.

GENERAL
▲ Curiosity, exploration, new ideas, enthusiasm.

▼ Lack of focus, impatience, unrealistic expectations.

LOVE
▲ Excitement, new beginnings, youthful energy in love.

▼ Lack of direction, immaturity, setbacks.

MONEY
▲ Curiosity, exploring new ideas, learning financial skills.

▼ Impatience, unrealistic expectations, rushing into investments.

CAREER
▲ Enthusiasm, curiosity, exploring new ideas, eager to learn new skills.

▼ Impatience, unrealistic expectations, neglecting foundational knowledge, making impulsive decisions.

HEALTH-WELLBEING
▲ Curiosity, exploring new approaches, learning healthy habits.

▼ Impatience, unrealistic expectations, neglecting sustainable changes.

SPIRITUALITY
▲ Spiritual exploration, new ideas, enthusiasm.

▼ Immaturity, lack of focus, missed opportunities.

COURT CARD | KNIGHT
Symbolize action, adventure, and movement.

KNIGHT of WANDS.

Knight of Wands

"ADVENTUROUS SPIRIT AND BOLD ACTION"
Depicting a knight on horseback with a wand, it symbolizes the pursuit of adventurous endeavors and taking swift, decisive action.

Michael
Archangel

Fire
Element

Plexus
Chakras

Spiritual
Domain

Diamonds
Traditional Cards

Action, passion, impulsiveness.	Confidence, charisma, adventure	Communication, dynamic expression.	Courage, creativity, spontaneity.
RED	**YELLOW**	**BLUE**	**ORANGE**

ARMOR AND GLOVES:
Preparedness for challenges.

YELLOW CLOAK:
Vibrant energy and enthusiasm.

SALAMANDERS:
Resilience and adaptability.

RED HORSE:
Symbol of strength and ambition.

PYRAMIDS:
Quest for wisdom and enlightenment.

ARID DESERT:
Confronting challenges on an adventurous journey.

GENERAL
▲ Action, adventure, leadership, initiative.

▼ Aggression, recklessness, pushing too hard.

LOVE
▲ Passion, adventure, boldness in love.

▼ Impulsiveness, recklessness, inconsistency.

MONEY
▲ Action, taking initiative, assertiveness, pursuing opportunities.

▼ Aggression, impulsiveness, taking unnecessary risks.

CAREER
▲ Action, initiative, assertiveness, advocating for career needs, taking risks.

▼ Aggression, impulsiveness, neglecting rest and planning, burning out.

HEALTH-WELLBEING
▲ Action, taking initiative, assertiveness, advocating for health needs.

▼ Aggression, impulsiveness, neglecting rest and recovery.

SPIRITUALITY
▲ Spiritual passion, adventure, pursuit.

▼ Recklessness, impulsiveness, lack of direction.

COURT CARD | QUEEN
Represent nurturing, authority, and intuition.

QUEEN of WANDS.

Queen of Wands

"CREATIVE LEADERSHIP AND VIBRANT ENERGY"
Depicting a queen with a sunflower throne and wand, it symbolizes the ability to lead with creativity and enthusiasm.

Michael *Archangel*	**Fire** *Element*	**Plexus** *Chakras*	**Spiritual** *Domain*	**Diamonds** *Traditional Cards*

YELLOW	RED	GREEN	BLACK
Confidence, warmth, generosity.	Leadership, passion, charisma.	Nurturing, growth, abundance.	Mystery, depth, power, authority, protection.

LION:
Strength and regal presence.

SUNFLOWERS:
Joy and vitality.

BLACK CAT:
Intuition and mystery.

WAND:
Creative energy and manifestation.

CROWN:
Authority and leadership.

PYRAMIDS:
Connection to ancient wisdom.

RED SHOE AND YELLOW DRESS:
Passion, confidence, and creativity.

GENERAL
▲ Confidence, self-reliance, creativity, inspiration.

▼ Domination, controlling, neglecting intuition.

LOVE
▲ Confidence, vibrancy, magnetic attraction.

▼ Jealousy, insecurity, domineering behavior.

MONEY
▲ Confidence, independence, resourcefulness, managing finances.

▼ Controlling, manipulative, neglecting long-term planning.

CAREER
▲ Confidence, independence, resourcefulness, managing career holistically, inspiring others.

▼ Dominance, manipulation, neglecting empathy, neglecting work-life balance.

HEALTH-WELLBEING
▲ Confidence, independence, resourcefulness, managing health holistically.

▼ Controlling, manipulative, neglecting emotional well-being.

SPIRITUALITY
▲ Spiritual charisma, confidence, leadership.

▼ Arrogance, manipulation, temperamental.

COURT CARD | KING
Symbolize mastery, authority, and control.

King of Wands

"CHARISMATIC LEADERSHIP AND MASTERY"
Depicting a king holding a wand and salamander throne, it symbolizes the ability to lead with charisma and mastery of one's domain.

Michael *Archangel* **Fire** *Element* **Plexus** *Chakras* **Spiritual** *Domain* **Diamonds** *Traditional Cards*

Confidence, optimism, creative vision. **YELLOW**

Leadership, passion, strength. **RED**

Spiritual insight, clarity, purpose, purity. **WHITE**

Communication, wisdom, dynamic leadership. **BLUE**

CROWN: Authority and regality.

YELLOW THRONE: Energy and optimism.

RED GOWN: Passion and dynamism.

SALAMANDERS: Resilience and transformation.

LIONS: Strength and courage.

GENERAL
▲ Authority, ambition, vision, stability.
▼ Tyranny, rigidity, clinging to power.

LOVE
▲ Leadership, vision, dynamic energy in relationships.
▼ Impatience, arrogance, controlling behavior.

MONEY
▲ Leadership, vision, stability, providing financial security.
▼ Tyranny, rigidity, clinging to wealth, neglecting ethical practices.

CAREER
▲ Vision, leadership, inspiration, providing guidance and support for others' careers.
▼ Domination, rigidity, neglecting collaboration, overlooking potential of others.

HEALTH-WELLBEING
▲ Leadership, stability, wisdom, providing support for others' health.
▼ Tyranny, rigidity, neglecting self-care, controlling others health.

SPIRITUALITY
▲ Spiritual leadership, vision, authority.
▼ Tyranny, domination, lack of control.

Also available on Ipad

Scan me

https://etsy.me/4btaOyp

Made in the USA
Las Vegas, NV
28 October 2024

10539101R00057